T0069362

New Testament Evangelism

Campaign Guide and Handbook

By C. J. SHARP

THE STANDARD PUBLISHING COMPANY
CINCINNATI, OHIO, U. S. A.

Such Scriptures as are used from the American Standard Edition of the Revised Bible, copyright, 1929, by International Council of Religious Education, are used by permission.

Printed in U. S. A.

Foreword

Forty years ago, J. V. Coombs, one of our most successful evangelists, prepared and gave to the brotherhood a little volume, called "Campaigning for Christ." It has been one of the most practically helpful books ever produced by one of our people. Very probably, every evangelistically-inclined minister in the brotherhood has at sometime read and profited by it. While that book had much of permanent value, yet in forty years it has somewhat run its normal course and is now out of print. Many have suggested that a new and fresh treatise is much needed.

In this book, "New Testament Evangelism," we attempt to bring together from the experiences of our own ministry, and from those of many of our outstandingly successful ministers and evangelists, a collection of the best tried plans. We have endeavored to crowd into small space everything possible that might be helpful to preachers, elders, teachers and leaders in planning for, preparing for, and carrying on an evangelistic campaign.

We have divided the book into four parts, under the general themes of, I. "The Why of Evangelism," II. "The How of Evangelism," III. "Ammunition for the Campaign," IV. "Care of the Converts." In addition, we have included, in the appendix, a number of miscellaneous, practical helps.

If every congregation planning for a meeting, whether it is to be conducted by a visiting evangelist or by home forces, would prepare as comprehensively as this little book suggests, there would be a blessing showered upon our churches by Him who giveth the increase.

[3]

How to Use This Book

This is not primarily a book to be read, but rather more to be used through many campaigns. We have attempted to condense and put in the hands of each, the combined experience of all. There are many practical ways in which this book may be used. We mention some of them:

1. Read it through for the purpose of familiarizing yourself with its plan and content. Mark it or make mental note of parts or sections you may want to use for any purpose at some future time.

2. While the whole book is not intended for a class study book, yet parts of it are intended to be so used, if desired. This would apply especially to Part III, Section A. All of Part I might profitably be so used in preparation for a meeting. Copies in the hands of all church officers and Bible-school workers prior to the meeting will be a great help.

3. Suggestions for reprints. Especially in Part III and in the Appendix, will be found materials which are intended as suggestions for reprint on charts, banners, or cards for various practical uses.

4. There is no thought that any one congregation should use everything suggested in the book for any one meeting. The book is intended to contain tried plans and suggestions which may be usable for some years.

5. While it is valuable for the minister to have these helps, it is of even greater value to him, and to the whole congregation, if a large number of leaders may be induced to secure and ponder copies of their own, for thus they will have not only a greater personal interest, but a liberal knowledge of tried and wise plans.

Index

Chapter	Page
Foreword	3
How to Use This Book	4

Part I. The Why of Evangelism

I.	Why Your Church Should Have a Revival This Year	7
II.	The Evangelistic Campaign, the Best Cure for Local Church Ills	10
III.	Evangelism the Best Cure for Brotherhood Problems	14
IV.	Present Day Need for the New Testament Message	16
V.	Jesus and Evangelism	19
VI.	The New Testament and Evangelism	22
VII.	Paul's Evangelism	26
VIII.	When Evangelism Halts, the Church Halts	29
IX.	Our Responsibility for the Unsaved	32
X.	Can Every Congregation Have a Revival Each Year?	36

Part II. The How of Evangelism

Section A. Preparing the Field for the Campaign

I.	Securing the Evangelist	40
II.	Setting the Building in Order	44
III.	Districting the Territory and Taking a Census	47
IV.	Music for the Evangelistic Campaign	51
V.	Ushers and Ushering	55
VI.	Practical Suggestions on Advertising	61
VII.	Publicity for the Campaign	67
VIII.	Calling: When, How and on Whom	70
IX.	Preparatory Doctrinal Teaching	75
X.	Financing the Campaign	78

Section B. Definite Work of the Campaign

I.	Preparing the Membership for the Campaign, in Spirituality, Interest, Incentive and Expectancy	87
II.	Planning and Conducting Cottage Prayer Meetings	93
III.	Securing and Using Prospect and Prayer Lists	98
IV.	The Minister's Work in Organization of the Forces and Assignment of Tasks	102

[5]

Index

V. Preparatory Work of the Elders and Bible-school Superintendent 106

VI. Men and the Campaign 110

VII. The Women's Work for the Campaign 114

VIII. Using the Youth of the Church 121

IX. Personal Work in the Campaign 124

X. The Use of Tracts in Evangelism 129

Part III. Ammunition for the Campaign

Explanation of Uses of Sections in Part III 132

Section A. Ten Brief Doctrinal Studies

I. The Bible and How to Present It 135

II. The Divine Plan 138

III. What Does God Require Us to Believe and Why? 141

IV. The Turning Point 143

V. The First Open Step—Confession 146

VI. Bible Facts About Baptism 149

VII. The Name, Does It Make Any Difference? 152

VIII. The Church, Why Belong to It? 154

IX. The Communion Service, Why Attend? 158

X. What Does God Require of Me as a Christian? 161

Section B. Doctrinal, Bible School, Opening Exercise.. 165

Section C. Doctrinal Charts and Drill 166

Part IV. Care of the Converts

I. The Responsibility and the Need 168

II. A Definite Plan 171

III. Oversight and Training by Elders and Minister 175

Appendix

Some Do's and Do-not's for the Campaign 178

Form of Religious Census 181

Forms of Cards for Personal Workers 182

Form of Card for Enrollment of Converts in Service and Giving 183

Doctrinal Drill for Children's Service 184

Baptismal Robe, Drawings and Specifications 187

Suggestions for Advertising 189

CHAPTER I.

WHY YOUR CHURCH SHOULD HAVE A REVIVAL THIS YEAR

"The Son of man is come to seek and to save that which was lost" (Luke 19:10). "As my Father hath sent me, even so send I you" (John 20: 21).

All that follows in the first ten chapters is but an answer to the proposition which heads this chapter, but a preliminary sketching is provided to prepare our minds and hearts for what is to follow.

Perhaps terms should first be made plain. We use the word "revival" in the old-fashioned sense of a "protracted meeting" or "evangelistic campaign." The latter term more nearly describes the work actually to be accomplished. The term "revival" has been in bad repute because too often connected with claptrap methods and psychologic manipulations known as "revivalism," rather than with clear teaching of the Word and sincere and earnest exhortation to accept and follow it. However, the word "revival" should not be wholly taboo, for it is a fact that there is no other plan so well suited to revive the church itself, as an aggressive campaign to carry the message to others.

[7]

Your congregation, and every congregation, therefore, should have a protracted evangelistic campaign this year for the following reasons:

(1) *To fulfill the church's purpose.* Thus we can well carry out the first reason for the church's existence; i. e., the preaching of the gospel to the unsaved.

(2) *To revive and re-educate members.* It meets the need for reviving, reinspiring and re-educating the members, young and old, in the basic terms of the gospel.

(3) *To focus on important things.* For the purpose of diverting attention from local ills, squabbles, misunderstandings, and from inconsequential things, to the really great and inspiring things of Christ and Christianity, such a campaign serves more effectively than any other plan that has been tried.

(4) *As a solution for brotherhood ills.* There is nothing so helpful for unifying the members of a congregation or for unifying our congregations as a brotherhood, as aggressive evangelism. Herein lies the best cure for any brotherhood ills.

(5) *To stem the tide of godlessness and sin.* Sin and indifference are perhaps more thoroughly entrenched and aggressive today than at any time in the past centuries. It is time for the army of God to attack.

(6) *To fulfill our Lord's purpose and command.* The church is not ours. It is Christ's. He founded it with and for a definite purpose. He said, "For the Son of man is come to seek and to save that which was lost" (Luke 19:10), and again, "As my Father hath sent me, even so send I you" (John 20:21), "Go ye therefore, and teach all nations, baptizing them in the name of the Father, and of the Son, and of the Holy Ghost" (Matt. 28:19). An aggressive evangelistic campaign fits exactly with these Scriptures.

[8]

(7) *To keep faith with our purpose as a New Testament people*. We claim to desire to be a New Testament people, restoring to the earth the ideal New Testament church. A large part of the Book of Acts is the record of the evangelism of Paul. Two-thirds of the Epistles are a further record of his work. Paul was first of all an evangelist. If we sincerely desire to restore New Testament Christianity we must restore New Testament evangelism.

(8) *To start a forward march*. A church which is not actively evangelizing is standing still. A church which is standing still is actually going backward. When evangelism and the evangelistic spirit halt, the church halts and souls that might be saved are lost.

(9) *A final reason*. A final reason why each congregation should have a protracted evangelistic campaign this year is that it *can* if it so desires. It is something that ought to be done, it is something that *can* be done, therefore it *should* be done. Plans whereby it may be accomplished constitute the whole purpose of this book.

(Each of these reasons is treated more at length in the pages immediately following.)

What We Desire Greatly

We Find a Way to Achieve.

What We Desire but Faintly

Can Be Easily Smothered by Excuses.

CHAPTER II

THE EVANGELISTIC CAMPAIGN, THE BEST CURE FOR LOCAL CHURCH ILLS

"Whatsoever things are true, whatsoever things are honest, whatsoever things are just, whatsoever things are pure, whatsoever things are lovely, whatsoever things are of good report; if there be any virtue, and if there be any praise, think on these things" (Phil. 4: 8).

Difficulties and Ills

Whatever hampers the church in doing the work of Christ in the community, hampers the Saviour and Lord who died for lost men. The church is Christ's one means and plan for carrying out His work in any given community. The church has to face two problems. They are: Difficulties, and what we term as "ills." The difficulties are from without. The ills are from within. Difficulties are natural and to be expected. The church can overcome all the difficulties if it can only overcome its ills.

What Some of the Ills Are

We may not be able to list all of the ills that afflict and hamper the church of the living God, but in general they would fall under: Indifference; lack of knowledge of the Word; lack of funds; divisions, squabbles and inharmony; positive sin and worldliness; lack of definite spiritual objective.

Spiritual Indifference

We believe that ministers and evangelists would testify, almost universally, that there is no other cure so effective for an indifferent membership as a well-planned, and well-directed evangelistic campaign. Even the "deadest" of the members show symptoms of life, and those who are alive receive a new inspiration that sets them to work with a quickened zeal. We may not know why, but it is an established psychological principle that working for others and for Christ dispels the deadening influence of indifference which is born of selfishness and self-interest. Not all spiritual indifference may be overcome, but a remarkable change is most surely to be found accompanying a good revival campaign.

Lack of Knowledge of the Word

With all our facilities for religious education it is almost unbelievable how very, very little of the Word of God the generality of church members knows. Indifference itself grows largely out of ignorance of the Word. The blighting hesitancy to try to lead another to Christ comes directly out of the consciousness of ignorance of the Word. Adults may sit in a Bible class and listen to lectures and discussions of many a page of Scripture, and none of it sink in far or stick. Practically none of it is put into action.

There is something about the night-after-night preaching and drilling in the Word that fixes at least some part of the Scriptures in the minds and hearts of people, and makes it theirs to practice and use. It may be only one Scripture that lays hold, but ofttimes one Scripture learned has transformed an indifferent member into a worker, or a disobedient person into a Christian. A properly conducted evangelistic campaign is a most effective school of intensive training in the Word, and therefore an antidote for the lack of knowledge of the Word, which is one of the church's severest ills.

[11]

Lack of Finances

Church boards, consisting of the chosen leaders of the congregation, too often meet and hesitate and adjourn, when any forward work of the church is proposed, because there is no surplus in sight to pay for the costs of the suggested forward move. The fact is that any wisely planned and conducted evangelistic meeting always generates the finances, not only to cover its own costs, but, because of the revived interest and the help of the newly added members, adds very materially to the current-expense income following the meeting. A good revival is the best of financial investments for any congregation. Any one with any considerable experience in raising financial budgets will testify that the easiest church money they are ever called upon to raise is that needed to cover the costs of a good evangelistic campaign.

Divisions and Inharmony

The devil finds work for idle hands. A group of people, even Christian people, who are not aggressively busy, can get into arguments over the smallest of things and develop real quarrels and divisions. Formulate a good evangelistic program, get all busy working to reach the unconverted and it is amazing how divisions, differences and enmities melt like frost before a summer sun. It is to be admitted that there is no more serious ill afflicting the church than these divisions and quarrels, but it is also true that the quickest, most effective and most lasting cure is to set all to work for the unsaved.

Positive Sin and Worldliness

From the beginning, the church has been afflicted by the weaknesses and sins of its members. Here lies one of its chief ills, and a chief stumblingblock for the ones we try to reach. No doubt this will be so to the end, but the fact remains that in innumerable cases a good revival meeting has quickened the spiritual life and conscience of the church members to the point of remarkable improvements in life and conduct. The gospel, listened to and worked for night after night, has transforming power as well as converting power.

Lack of Spiritual Objective

One of the severest ills of a very large percentage of congregations is the lack of a clear-cut, clearly-defined and worth-while program or objective. Week after week, month after month and year after year they go through with a mere routine, monotonous in its make-up and with no conscious goal. In a well-planned evangelistic meeting, every member is made aware of a definite aim and goal, at least temporarily, and also aware of the need for such a definite objective in the whole program of the year. Here is where wise leadership, or lack of it, shows.

In Faith Unity

In Obedience Loyalty

In Opinions Liberty

In All Things Charity

CHAPTER III

EVANGELISM THE BEST CURE FOR
BROTHERHOOD PROBLEMS

"So we, being many, are one body in Christ, and every one
members one of another" (Rom. 12: 5).

Unity a Brotherhood Need

Problems are not necessarily ills, but they may become so if difference of opinion leads to division and
disharmony in seeking their solution. A united and
harmonious brotherhood is certainly most desirable,
especially for a people who have set themselves to plead
for the unity of all Christ's followers in Christ and
on Christ.

The Sources of Disharmony

Such problems as we have faced as a brotherhood
have grown out of two things; one is our attempt to
formulate machinery for gathering money and directing a
world-wide missionary program, and the other grows
out of extreme, modernistic teachings which some have
attempted to make a part of our message. The radi-
cally modernistic viewpoint practically eschews what we
ordinarily recognize as evangelism, whereas evangelism
has found that modernism has no practical place in its
work or program. In actual practice, the two have
shown themselves to be mutually exclusive. When one
comes in the other goes out. It works both ways. Unless
there is in the Bible a God-given message, then Evangelism has no message to preach.

The Best Cure

If modernism be a prominent, contributing cause to lack of unity in the brotherhood, and therefore an ill in the brotherhood, its best antidote in any local situation is evangelism, i.e., an abundant and effective preaching of the Word. This is, or should be, the outstanding feature of every evangelistic campaign. While theories, philosophies and such like may appeal to the erudite and self-satisfied, there is nothing there to lay hold upon the lost sinner and turn him from indifference to a humble and contrite repentance. It is only a knowledge of God's love and of the consequences of sin that can do that.

As to such inharmonies as may grow purely out of differences of opinion as to methods and means by which the commission of our Lord and Saviour may best be carried out in getting His Word to all men at home and abroad, the plea which we preach provides for that. "In matters of faith, unity; in matters of obedience, loyalty; in matters of opinion, liberty; and in all things, charity."

Our Gospel Is a Unifying Gospel

The actual message which we preach, and the incentive to strive to win others has always warmed our hearts and unified us. When we all go actively to work to win the unsaved on every hand, we speedily relegate methods and means to their proper place of relative unimportance, and work together as brethren, rejoicing in the victories for Christ. Some things may divide us, but a brotherhood-wide restoration of aggressive evangelism will bind us together again.

CHAPTER IV

PRESENT-DAY NEED FOR THE NEW TESTAMENT MESSAGE

"And an highway shall be there, . . . and it shall be called The way of holiness; . . . the wayfaring men, though fools, shall not err therein" (Isa. 35: 8).

The Need in Days Past

We all admit that the simple New Testament message was sorely needed in the day of Campbell and Stone, when sectarian lines and bitterness were so strong that Christ's people were divided into camps so antagonistic that Christ was put to shame and His church stood stagnant.

An Urgent Need Today

While that condition may have changed very materially for the better, other conditions have arisen which produce a more urgent need for the simple, plain, God-given message. Where men were then in fog and confusion, due to sectarian division and bitterness, they are in a denser fog today, produced by philosophies and theories, and confusion confounded. Hundreds of cults, social-uplift schemes, materialistic programs of uplift and rabid atheistic propagandas thrust themselves upon the scene until men despair of knowing where to seek the truth. They turn to cynic indifference and fill their lives with worldly pleasures.

People, generally, are totally unaware that there is a simple, beautiful, understandable and God-given way of life that lends absolute assurance and guidance. If ever the plain preaching of the simple New Testament was needed, it is now.

Needed for the Sake of Sinners

Men are weary with confusion and darkness, but endure it because they have never seen the light. It is only with humility that we dare ponder on how many millions of people, who are now indifferent to Christ and the gospel, would turn gladly to Him if they should but come to know the simple terms of pardon so clearly given in the New Testament. In every community, however intelligent the people may be, there are great numbers who know nothing of the plain New Testament way of salvation.

Saints Need the Plea

There are two groups of saints who need to hear the old and eternal truths thundered forth with clarity and conviction. First, there are great hosts of our own brethren whose knowledge of the truth is so meager that it is pathetic and hopelessly weak. These need to be confirmed, strengthened and built up in the faith. Then there are the uncounted thousands of conscientious souls who have never heard any other than a denominational message and who are far from satisfied with it. They have sincerely followed the best light they have had, but would, and do, grasp avidly at the plain and Scriptural message when they hear it. The testimony of thousands who have found the more perfect way of the Lord is sufficient proof of this.

The Wandering Sheep Need the Plea

A third group is a large one indeed, and, perhaps, the most difficult of all. These are they who are immersed believers in Christ and one time held membership somewhere. They have sometimes been called "trunk members" because they are supposed to have unpresented church letters locked in their trunks. It is even worse than this, however, for ninety-nine out of a hundred of them have moved from their old church homes and have never even taken the trouble to secure letters. They are just sheep astray. Some have drifted back into godless lives, some are merely cooled off and need to be warmed over, and some will welcome assistance to find again their places in the life of the church. All these one-time saints need the Word. Nothing else can help them.

The Best of Us Need the Teaching

Being self-satisfied by knowing and obeying the gospel terms is far from the New Testament ideal. The New Testament makes it pronouncedly plain, that we can not stand before the throne guiltless if we have failed to warn the unsaved. We ourselves need the influence of a thoroughgoing evangelistic campaign to warm, and thrill, and inspire, and fire us to service for Him in seeking the lost.

The Great Commission
Has Not Yet Been Amended.
It Still Says
"Go Ye."

CHAPTER V

JESUS AND EVANGELISM

"I must work the works of him that sent me, while it is day: the night cometh, when no man can work" (John 9: 4).

What Is an Evangelist?

An evangelist is a messenger and, according to the dictionary, means "a first announcer or preacher of the gospel." The gospel is the good news about the Saviour. In that sense any and every Christian can well be, and in reason should be, an evangelist. To confine the term merely to, "a preacher with no fixed charge who conducts revival meetings," is a much more modern use of the term than is comprehended in the New Testament.

It is with poor grace and little understanding that we go about wearing the name "Christian," claiming to be members of the church of Christ, and followers of Christ, if we miss, overlook or disregard the whole purpose of the coming of Him whom we claim to follow.

Jesus, the First Evangelist

Jesus was a messenger, the first bearer of the "good news" from God to man. He made His purpose plain: "For the Son of man is come to seek and to save that which was lost." He made plain to His followers what their first and primary task should be: "As my Father hath sent me, even so send I you." He made it plain that this message was for all: "Go ye therefore, and teach *all* nations."

[19]

Jesus Prepared Himself

Strange as it may seem, even the Son of God and Saviour most carefully prepared Himself for His task. He counted it the most important thing in the world, and approached it accordingly. He prepared Himself by acquiring:

(1) A complete knowledge of the then-existing divine Word. He so familiarized Himself with the Old Testament writings that they were at ever-ready command. Not only could He quote these Scriptures, as did the scribes and Pharisees, but He penetrated to and correctly presented their spiritual meaning and significance, where the scribes but taught their legalistic forms.

(2) He prepared Himself by prayer and direct communion with the Father so that when He came before the people to tell them of the heavenly Father, He came not as a ranting egotist, but as One who, it was evident, had just been in the Father's presence.

(3) Jesus prepared Himself by using His every faculty to familiarize Himself thoroughly with nature. He never lacked for apt, clear illustration drawn from things with which His hearers were entirely familiar.

(4) He prepared Himself by coming to know men and women in their everyday life. He understood people. He could enter sympathetically into their heartbreaks and understandingly into their weaknesses.

Jesus Prepared His Hearers for His Message

Jesus' approach to men was very tactful. His message not only brought the truth, but it is apparent that He kept in mind that the truth was presented, not for its own sake, but purely for the help it might bring to men.

Therefore, Jesus prepared His hearers. Note how He approached and prepared the heart and mind of the Samaritan woman at Jacob's well (John 4:4-26), or the minds of His disciples for the truth of His divine Sonship on their journey to Cæsarea Philippi (Matt. 16:13-19).

Jesus Trained Others to Carry On

Jesus was as careful to choose and train others to carry His work and message on as He was in all else He did. It is quite as much the work of evangelists, preachers, elders and Christians in general to train others most carefully, as it is to win them to Christ. Jesus not only gave us the truth which we are to promulgate, but He gave us the finest of examples of how best to promulgate it. If we would be successful evangelists, whether public, professional, personal, or of whatever kind, we can make no better preparation than to study carefully, again and again, the attitudes, methods and examples given us by the great Evangelist, Jesus the Christ.

"The Son of Man is Come
to Seek and to Save that which was Lost."
"As My Father Hath Sent Me,
Even so Send I You."

---

[21]

CHAPTER VI

THE NEW TESTAMENT AND EVANGELISM

"And the Spirit and the bride say, Come. And let him that heareth say, Come. And let him that is athirst come. And whosoever will, let him take the water of life freely" (Rev. 22: 17).

A New Testament People Can Not Avoid Being Evangelistic

A New Testament people, who are truly a New Testament people, can not possibly be anything else than intensely evangelistic. They will not be unduly afraid of numbers. In fact, their convictions will be so positive, their earnestness so pronounced, their love so great, their zeal so persistent, and their efforts so general, that large numbers are bound to hear and heed.

Evangelism as Pictured in the New Testament

If one who is the least inclined to disparage the reaching of great numbers of people, but who yet claims kindred with a people set to restore the New Testament church, with its doctrines, its fruits and its ordinances, will but consult the New Testament on the subject, he will be amazed as well as convinced. Nothing we can offer in this line is so convincing as the New Testament itself. We here present only a part of the Scriptures that may be found on the subject in but two of the New Testament books, Matthew and Acts.

In preparing for an evangelistic campaign, we know of no better sermon to help create a proper atmosphere than one which includes these Scriptures to be read *in toto* to the whole congregation. Or these Scriptures might be printed and distributed to the members.

Matthew

Hear the New Testament as recorded by Matthew:

"Then went out to him [John] **Jerusalem, and all Judæa, and all the region round about Jordan,** And were baptized of him in Jordan, confessing their sins" (Matt. 3: 5, 6).

"Then cometh Jesus from Galilee to Jordan unto John, to be baptized of him" (Matt. 3: 13).

"And he saith unto them, Follow me, and I will make you **fishers of men**" (Matt. 4: 19).

"And Jesus went about **all Galilee,** teaching in their synagogues, and preaching the gospel of the kingdom" (Matt. 4: 23).

"And there followed him **great multitudes of people** from **Galilee,** and from **Decapolis,** and from **Jerusalem,** and from **Judea,** and from **beyond Jordan**" (Matt. 4: 25).

"When he was come down from the mountain, **great multitudes followed him**" (Matt. 8: 1).

"And, behold, the **whole city came out** to meet Jesus" (Matt. 8: 34).

"But when the **multitudes** saw it, they marvelled, and glorified God" (Matt. 9: 8).

"**Many publicans and sinners** came and sat down with him and his disciples" (Matt. 9: 10).

"And Jesus went about **all the cities and villages,** teaching in their synagogues" (Matt. 9: 35).

"But when he saw the **multitudes,** he was moved with compassion on them, because they fainted, and were scattered abroad, as sheep having no shepherd" (Matt. 9: 36).

"Then saith he unto his disciples, The **harvest truly is plenteous,** but the **laborers are few;** Pray ye therefore the Lord of the harvest, that he will send forth laborers into his harvest" (Matt. 9: 37, 38).

"What I tell you in darkness, that speak ye in light: and what ye hear in the ear, **that preach ye upon the housetops**" (Matt. 10: 27).

[23]

"And **great multitudes** were gathered together unto him, so that he went into a ship, and sat; and the **whole multitude stood on the shore**" (Matt. 13: 2).

"And Jesus went forth, and saw a **great multitude**" (Matt. 14: 14).

"And he commanded the **multitude** to sit down . . . And they that had eaten were about **five thousand men,** beside women and children" (Matt. 14: 19, 21).

"And when the men of that place had knowledge of him, they sent out **into all that country round about,** and brought unto him all that were diseased" (Matt. 14: 35).

"And **great multitudes** came unto him" (Matt. 15: 30).

"And **great multitudes** followed him; and he healed them there" (Matt. 19: 2).

"And a **very great multitude** spread their garments in the way; . . . And **the multitudes that went before, and that followed,** cried, saying, Hosanna to the son of David" (Matt. 21: 8, 9).

"**All the city** was moved" (Matt. 21: 10).

"Go ye therefore **into the highways**" (Matt. 22: 9).

Hear the Record in Acts

"And the same day there were added unto them about **three thousand souls**" (Acts 2: 41).

"Howbeit **many of them** which heard the word believed; and the number of the men was about **five thousand**" (Acts 4: 4).

"And the **multitude of them that believed** were of one heart and of one soul" (Acts 4: 32).

"And **believers were the more added** to the Lord, **multitudes** both of men and women" (Acts 5: 14).

"There came also a **multitude out of the cities** round about" (Acts 5: 16).

"And the **word of God increased;** and the **number** of the disciples **multiplied** in Jerusalem greatly; and a **great company** of the priests were obedient to the faith" (Acts 6: 7).

"They that were scattered abroad went **every where** preaching the word" (Acts 8: 4).

"And the **people with one accord** gave heed unto those things which Philip spake" (Acts 8: 6).

"To whom they **all gave heed, from the least to the greatest,** . . . they were baptized, both men and women" (Acts 8: 10, 12).

[24]

"And straightway he [Saul], **preached Christ in the synagogues**" (Acts 9: 20).

"All that dwelt at **Lydda** and **Saron** saw him [Peter], and turned to the Lord" (Acts 9: 35).

"Now they which were scattered abroad upon the persecution . . . travelled as far as **Phenice**, and **Cyprus**, and **Antioch**, preaching the word" (Acts 11: 19).

"**A great number believed,** and turned unto the Lord" (Acts 11: 21).

"The word of God **grew and multiplied**" (Acts 12: 24).

"The next sabbath day came **almost the whole city** together to hear the word of God" (Acts 13: 44).

"And the word of the Lord was published **throughout all the region**" (Acts 13: 49).

"**A great multitude** both of the **Jews** and also of the **Greeks** believed" (Acts 14: 1).

"And so were the churches established in the faith, and **increased in number daily** (Acts 16: 5).

"And some of them believed, . . . and of the devout Greeks **a great multitude,** and of the **chief women not a few**" (Acts 17: 4).

"These that have **turned the world upside down** are come hither also" (Acts 17: 6).

Not the Numbers But the Motive

Most certainly numbers are not to be sought for vain glory, personal aggrandizement, false pride or party prestige. But the fact remains that New Testament precedent calls for large numbers to be sought and reached. We need only to safeguard our motive. Our motive should grow out of the facts that the unsaved are lost, that Christ is their only hope, the gospel is their only guide and Christians are Christ's only dependence to preach the gospel.

CHAPTER VII

PAUL'S EVANGELISM

"I am made all things to all men, that I might by all means save some" (1 Cor. 9: 22).

A Real New Testament Evangelist

Again we should call to mind our aim to be a New Testament people set to restore the ideal New Testament church. As we go to the New Testament for guidance in evangelism, we come face to face with the most outstanding Christian evangelist of all time. Whether we study the man, his message or his methods we are facing evangelism *par excellence*. The larger part of the Book of Acts is but the record of Paul's evangelism, and two-thirds of all the Epistles are but further records of his work. We speak and think of Paul as a "missionary" and divide his work into missionary periods or journeys, but that is a somewhat modern term for what was looked upon by Paul as "evangelism." No distinction should be made. Our task is to evangelize all people who are not evangelized, whether at home or abroad. This was Paul's view.

Paul, a Man of Passion

Paul so appreciated what forgiveness and salvation through Christ meant to him, that he was determined to throw his every power and energy into service for Christ. This accounts for his driving force, determination, patience and persistence.

He was a herald of the gospel, a man with whom the turning of men to Christ was a passion. He was tremendously in earnest, and his earnestness was plainly apparent. Earnestness begets fervor. The word "fervor" comes from the same root as "fire"! It takes fire to start fire. A cold, logical presentation of gospel facts is better than the presentation of something that is not the gospel. However, cold facts may convince, but seldom convict or inspire. We are to be "fervent in spirit; serving the Lord." One great Scriptural truth presented with a passion is more liable to melt the barriers of indifference than would be a hundred Scriptures coldly presented.

Paul Knew the Scriptures

Paul was the most logical expounder of the Old Testament Scriptures that has ever lived except only Jesus Himself. Paul balanced his passion with knowledge and his knowledge with passion. Men by hundreds were led to accept Christ when it meant the sacrifice of every associate and the almost sure risk of life. Paul convinced and then convicted. Men, reared in heathenism, surrounded by heathenism and steeped in heathen customs and philosophy were led to accept the Christ and the standards of Christian living. Many became examples of Christian living for all time to come. Paul *grounded them* in the gospel. This is evangelism indeed.

Paul Became All Things to All Men

There is much in the little word "all." One of our most difficult tasks is the task of adjusting ourselves to the many and varying kinds of people who are unsaved; the rich and poor, the educated and the ignorant, the cultured and the very uncultured, the farmer and the city

[27]

dweller, the happy and the unhappy, the young and the old, the earnest and the frivolous, the clean and the unclean, the repentant and the unrepentant. Paul set us the example, and the responses he obtained, from the servant of Philemon on one hand and members of the household of Cæsar on the other, lead us to believe it paid thus to become all things to all men.

Paul Worked

To win the world to Christ takes work. In fact, it takes work, real work, many times to win just one for Him. An evangelistic campaign means work, work, extra work on the part of the preacher, before the meeting, during the meeting and after the meeting. It likewise means work on the part of the members. This may be one reason for the unpopularity of the evangelistic campaigns in some places. Consecrated feet are seriously needed if the unsaved are to be reached. If we study Paul as an example we can not help being amazed at the amount of hard traveling he did and at the physical energy and endurance which he showed. But what a reward he had! "Beautiful are the feet of them that preach the gospel of peace."

Paul Took a Personal Interest in People

The gospel is holy, sacred and divinely inspired and yet it is, after all, but a means to an end. The end sought is that men may be saved. With all Paul's fervor, logic and eloquence, he never became enthralled by his logic nor enamored of his eloquence. He was willing to sacrifice either at a moment's notice to win another to Christ.

[28]

CHAPTER VIII

WHEN EVANGELISM HALTS, THE CHURCH HALTS

"I know thy works, that thou hast a name that thou livest, and art dead" (Rev. 3: 1).

The head of this chapter states a truism which scarcely needs explanation or delineation. A congregation may cease to grow numerically and yet continue to increase in wealth, social prestige and the general status of worldly culture. It may at the same time be making no forward progress as a church of Christ.

A Delusion Dissipated

There has also been a delusion spread abroad that a church may have either an evangelistic program or a program calculated to build up the spiritual life of the members, but that the two programs have little in common and are practically mutually exclusive. We believe this to be decidedly untrue. Is the real spirituality of a given group of Christians best enhanced by definitely planning to discontinue active efforts to win others to Christ in order to concentrate on self? Is it true that a general spirit of working to lead others to Christ is devoid of spiritualizing influence? Is it not true that every one of us are actually more benefited spiritually by what we do for others, in prayer, in teaching, and in leading, than by merely concentrating on our own soul's spiritual development? Is it not the experience of ministers and evangelists that a busy people, busy about the

Lord's work, are bound to be growing in spirituality more rapidly and more certainly than an inactive group?

What Is a Spiritual Church?

What is a spiritual church? Is it a group that has merely cultivated a pious face; a soft voice; a superior attitude toward others; an undue longing for popularity from without; an appetite that calls only for milk and gags at meat; a nice, clubby, mutual-admiration atmosphere; and a closed-corporation complex toward the unwashed and unregenerated, is that the really spiritual church?

Shall the Church Function or Merely Exist?

Granted the soul-soothing satisfaction of filtered light and of set, ritualistic services of worship, and granted the extreme desirability of order and beauty in Christian worship, if these things are gained at the expense of the church's losing sight of its first purpose to evangelize the unevangelized, then the price has been far too great. Granted the almost universal longing to be lulled, it yet remains a fact that our Book says, in the words of Jesus, "I must work the works of him that sent me, while it is day: the night cometh, when no man can work." Our interest as "Christians only" should be not merely to *maintain a church,* but to *constitute a church of Christ* which is a church of Christ in deed as well as in name.

The Marching Orders Still Hold

With two-thirds of the world still in total ignorance of the gospel of Christ; with exactly half of the youth of school age in America, that is to say with seventeen millions of boys and girls in age between four and eighteen years, totally untouched by and untaught in the Bible, in either Protestant or Catholic church schools; with sixty-four millions of the total population of America wholly unaligned with any kind of church accepting Christ as Saviour, as against sixty-three millions who claim membership in churches, it is no time for the church to halt in its forward march. The marching orders yet hold. The Great Commission is quite as much in effect today as it was when Jesus uttered it.

> "One Lord, One Faith
> One Baptism
> One God and Father
> Over All"

CHAPTER IX

OUR RESPONSIBILITY FOR THE UNSAVED

"And the lord said unto the servant, Go out into the highways and hedges, and compel them to come in, that my house may be filled" (Luke 14: 23).

We Shall Answer for More Than Ourselves

We Christians too often live under the delusion that we shall answer only for our own selves. The Bible makes it plain that there is somewhat more for which we must answer. Christians are responsible for those out of Christ *if they have not been warned*. We shall not be responsible for whether men yield to Christ, but we shall most certainly be responsible if we have failed to warn them. Hear the Scriptures:

"Son of man, I have made thee a watchman unto the house of Israel: therefore hear the word at my mouth, and give them warning from me. When I say unto the wicked, Thou shalt surely die; and thou givest him not warning, nor speakest to warn the wicked from his wicked way, to save his life; the same wicked man shall die in his iniquity; but his blood will I require at thine hand. Yet if thou warn the wicked, and he turn not from his wickedness, nor from his wicked way, he shall die in his iniquity; but thou hast delivered thy soul. Again, When a righteous man doth turn from his righteousness, and commit iniquity, and I lay a stumblingblock before him, he shall die: because thou hast not given him warning, he shall die in his sin, and his righteousness which he hath done shall not be remembered; but his blood will I require at thine hand. Nevertheless if thou warn the righteous man, that the righteous sin not, and he doth not sin, he shall surely live, because he is warned; also thou hast delivered thy soul" (Ezek. 3: 17-21).

"And they that be wise shall shine as the brightness of the firmament; and they that turn many to righteousness as the stars for ever and ever" (Dan. 12: 3).

"Let him know, that he which converteth the sinner from the error of his way shall save a soul from death, and shall hide a multitude of sins" (Jas. 5: 20).

The Great Commission Is to All

In the development of Christianity through the ages, it penetrated many lands and encountered every kind of pagan custom and religion. Quite a number of practices were absorbed from heathen religions. One of the developments picked up from heathenism was the practice of priestcraft and a strictly clerical class. The distinction as between clergy and laity that persists today, not only among Catholics but among Protestants, is one wholly unprovided for in the New Testament. Truly the New Testament provides for elders or bishops, spiritual overseers of the flock, for deacons or servants, and for evangelists and teachers, but all these are counted as but brethren with special duties and obligations assigned. "One is your Master, even Christ; and all ye are brethren" (Matt. 23: 8).

Why We Pass By on the Other Side

This, no doubt, is one of the reasons why the ordinary Christian can read the Great Commission and pass it by with no feeling of responsibility. Subconsciously we feel that this is a command to a clergy and does not apply to us.

As a matter of fact, when Jesus said, "Go ye into all the world, and preach the gospel to every creature," He was speaking to every follower of His in every clime and for all time. Some may go to Africa, or India, or China, and I may even help to send them, but this in no sense excuses me from going to some, in some part of the world —my part of the world—and endeavoring to turn them to Christ and salvation through Him. The "Go ye" is to me.

Paul's Example

Paul said, "I am debtor both to the Greeks, and to the Barbarians; both to the wise, and to the unwise." Paul felt that he owed a tremendous debt for the forgiveness and salvation which was his through Christ. This debt was wholly impossible for him to pay directly to the Christ. The same is true of us all. The only way Paul or we can pay the debt we owe is by counting that we owe it to the unsaved to carry to them the knowledge of the gospel.

A General Responsibility

It is easy for even so good an institution as Christianity to drift into system and become stereotyped and professionalized. The church *hires* a minister to serve the members. They make it plain that his responsibility is to them. In a sense it is, provided they keep in mind their responsibilty to Christ and the unsaved.

The fact is that the minister is responsible to and for the unsaved. The church is responsible to and for the unsaved. The members are responsible to and for the unsaved. Like Paul, we are debtor to them.

An Excellent Way to Pay the Debt

We can, one by one, learn how to go to others personally so that every one, in our community at least, has been warned. However, a somewhat easier and more effective way is for all to work together in harmony, move in concert, choose a skilled leader, divide the tasks and

[34]

attack the problems as a community of workers. This would be the organized evangelistic meeting. When all work, it helps the courage of each; it increases the incentive of each, and the inspiration becomes mutual. Also, it is true that such a concerted move arouses the community, gets the unsaved to thinking and helps amazingly to open the people's hearts for the gospel truth. Every congregation of Christ's followers should conduct at least one such concerted campaign each year.

New Testament Scriptures on the Subject

The proposition that men without Christ are lost is borne out in the New Testament.

"For all have sinned, and come short of the glory of God" (Rom. 3: 23).

"No man cometh unto the Father, but by me" (John 14: 6).

"But without faith it is impossible to please him" (Heb. 11: 6).

"For the wages of sin is death" (Rom. 6: 23).

"Except ye repent, ye shall all likewise perish" (Luke 13: 3).

"Repent, and be baptized every one of you in the name of Jesus Christ for the remission of sins" (Acts 2: 38).

"There is therefore now no condemnation to them which are in Christ Jesus" (Rom. 8: 1).

"For as many of you as have been baptized into Christ have put on Christ" (Gal. 3: 27).

"The blood of Jesus Christ his Son cleanseth us from all sin" (1 John 1:7).

Where the Bible Speaks

We Speak

Where the Bible Is Silent

We Are Silent

CHAPTER X

CAN EVERY CONGREGATION HAVE A REVIVAL EACH YEAR?

"And this is the victory that overcometh the world, even our faith" (1 John 5: 4).

Where the Answer Lies

Can every Christian congregation have a revival meeting this year? We answer "yes" and "no." They most certainly can if they sincerely and earnestly desire such a meeting, and have for their motive the reaching of the unsaved. Our answer is that they positively can not if they are more interested in their congregational glory and prestige than they are in the fact that more than half the people in America are out of Christ.

In this brief chapter it will be impossible to go fully into just how it can be done. However, we shall go far enough, even here, to attempt to prove that *each congregation CAN* if they so desire. The HOW of each phase will be discussed at considerably more length in the various chapters of Part II of this book.

The Evangelists Are Available

There are easily one hundred or more evangelists among us who devote their whole time to such meetings. Each of these is capable of conducting at least twelve meetings a year on the average. This will take care of twelve hundred congregations. While it is true that there

are some unworthy or inadvisable men posing as evangelists, there is a great host who are wholly worthy. All
that needs to be done is to take great care in choosing
the evangelist. Start now, plan ahead, choose a man
who is, first of all, worthy and dependable. Choose one
who by his experience is suited to your field, and whose
financial needs and plans are in keeping with your possi-
bilities. Evangelists have various financial plans suitable
to any field. Put all these evangelists to work.

Minister Evangelists

We have about five thousand employed ministers. A
very large proportion of these are evangelistic, and can
secure permission from their congregations to get away for
a meeting in another field each year. Many of them are
glad to do so. In fact, every employed minister ought to
get out of his own field and hold a meeting in at least
one other field each year. Every congregation ought to
be glad to have its minister do so. Again the financial
plans are various and suited to any and all fields, small
as well as large.

The Volunteer Evangelist

There is an ever-growing number of our ministers in
all states who are willing to contribute their services to
conduct meetings for congregations that are actually
unable to pay for these services. Nearly one thousand such
meetings were conducted in one year, recently. Many
states have lists of these ministers who have offered this
service. Their churches agree to continue their salaries
while they are absent helping to plant a new church or
reopen a closed church, or build up a weakened church,
in some outlying community.

[37]

Gospel Team Meetings

Within the past few years, there has developed a work in many congregations through which gospel teams of laymen have gone out and conducted excellent evangelistic campaigns for smaller outlying churches.

The Home-Force Meeting

It is only a few years since the average minister thought he could not conduct a revival, but must secure the leadership of a professional evangelist. In the past few years, most of our ministers have learned the technique of organizing their congregations and leading them in good, home-force meetings.

With all the above-mentioned preaching resources available, it is quite possible for every congregation, large or small, to have a good revival this year, so far as evangelists are concerned.

The Financing Is No Hindrance

As we have said before, a properly conducted revival is never a financial liability, but is a financial asset to the whole work of the congregation. Mistakes have been made, and can be made, but there is no excuse for the finance problem being any problem at all in planning for a meeting. The plans for it should be very definitely determined, and the best local man for the job made chairman of a revival, special-finance committee. The money for a good revival is the easiest of all church money to raise. It is not usually at all necessary to have the money costs raised or even pledged before the meeting starts. It is easier, and usually much wiser, to provide only what may be absolutely necessary in preliminary expenses, then bend every effort toward making

[38]

the meeting a success, merely taking a strictly freewill offering each night. When the meeting is nicely under way, there will be enough interest aroused to bring money in that would not even have been thought of before the meeting started. The plan must be determined by the local circumstances, and by such plans as the evangelist may suggest. Much more in detail, on this subject, will be found in Part II of this book. The thought here is that it is always possible to finance a properly planned evangelistic meeting. The meeting can be held, so far as finances are concerned. Have faith and go ahead.

**It Takes a Large List
of Excuses to Alibi for
the Natural Laziness
of All of Us**

PART II
The How of Evangelism
Section A. *Preparing the Field for the Campaign*

CHAPTER I

SECURING THE EVANGELIST

"But watch thou in all things, endure afflictions, do the work of an evangelist, make full proof of thy ministry" (2 Tim. 4: 5).

Search Early for the Suitable Leader

We treat this subject first in the discussion because it is quite often advisable to take up the matter of securing the evangelist a year in advance. There are some things that need to be taken into consideration in all cases where the congregation plans to employ a professional evangelist. May we say that there is an unjustified prejudice against all evangelists in some communities because among evangelists employed in time past the congregation failed to use due care in its choice, and unfortunately secured an unworthy man, or one wholly unsuited to the congregation and the community.

Take plenty of time to search out the evangelist who is not only unquestionably worthy in life, but whose tactics, costs and methods are acceptable in your pulpit and community. There are many available and wholly worthy evangelists.

Who Not to Secure

What we say here in the way of warning will not harm any worthy man, and such will rather welcome than resent it. First of all, do not employ, contract with, nor sanction the use of your pulpit by the stranger who simply drops in, claims to be a Christian evangelist, and agrees to hold a meeting for whatever may be thrown into the baskets, unless you have opportunity to know well the man with whom you are dealing, or unless he bears thoroughly up-to-date and unquestioned credentials from sources known to you. The church is Christ's, and the most sacred obligation in the world is the obligation of elders to safeguard the flock and the church. The life of the church, or the souls of the saved as well as the unsaved may be at stake. There are unworthy men posing as evangelists who are ruinous to the church, a menace to the cause of evangelism and an embarrassment and hindrance to all worthy evangelists. It is your duty to help safeguard against scoundrels who would prey on the church.

Know Many Worthy Evangelists

A wrong extreme is for ministers and elders to eschew all evangelists because there are counterfeits and misfits. We believe it is the duty of all ministers and elders to know scores of the many worthy and acceptable men. Every elder, in every church, should read at least the news reports of one or more of our church journals every week, until he is thoroughly conversant with a large number of the men engaged in evangelism. Ignorance of these things on the part of men honored by being made the spiritual pilots of churches is unnecessary, inexcusable and a reproach. Certainly your congregation is going to have many evangelistic meetings in the years to follow. Certainly you are going to be called upon to help to choose evangelists. Every elder should be capable of naming a dozen good evangelists, any one of whom could conduct a good meeting in the particular church in which the elder serves.

Take Time to Choose

Plan the meeting well ahead of time. Choose the time suited to your community and your people. Open correspondence and, before deciding upon your evangelist, ask for unquestioned credentials and references. Have a clear and clean-cut understanding as to the amount or plan of remuneration, the plan of financing, matters of entertainment, traveling expenses, publicity and advertising bills, etc. A clear-cut understanding is always best. Misunderstandings and ruined meetings are likely to result unless there is a clear understanding.

Consider Suitableness as Well as Success

Among the many good and successful evangelists there is a wide variety. A man who may be eminently suited to, and successful in, one community may not be the type that will appeal in your community. This again is an argument for choosing carefully, taking time, and for full familiarity with as large a number of evangelists as possible. One should be familiar with all the church-journal reports of evangelistic meetings, but should not depend on these alone. It is legitimate to seek all reliable sources of information in choosing the man who is to lead you in a soul-saving campaign. What we have said of choosing evangelists applies to the choice of song evangelists or other helpers. Not one word we have said here is intended to create distrust of our evangelists as a group,

[42]

but rather to encourage every congregation to make a much larger use of our many worthy evangelists.

Sources for Securing Evangelists

As said in a former chapter, every Christian congregation both can and should have one systematic soul-saving campaign each year, aside from the regular work of Bible school and other regular services. We ought to be evangelizing to the extent, not only that every one of our worthy men would be kept busy, but so that many, many more of our successful evangelistic ministers would be encouraged to enter the field for full-time evangelistic work.

Aside from our more than a hundred evangelists, we have many hundreds of employed ministers who can be secured for meetings. Our churches are beginning to see the advantage as well as the obligation of releasing their ministers for at least one meeting elsewhere each year.

Even the Least

For the church that is really too weak financially to secure an evangelist from one of the above sources, bear in mind that now some hundreds of churches have adopted the policy of loaning their ministers, salary guaranteed, or even salary paid, so that they may hold meetings in unentered or really weak centers.

Add to this the fact that we have also a very considerable number of gospel bands, gospel teams or lay evangelists who hold good meetings, but who, like Paul, make most of their living in business or some one of the professions, and it is apparent that any congregation can secure evangelistic leadership.

[43]

CHAPTER II

SETTING THE BUILDING IN ORDER

"For the stone shall cry out of the wall, and the beam out of the timber shall answer it" (Hab. 2: 11).

Material Equipment Influences Spiritual Results

Setting the building of the house of God in order in preparation for the revival may seem to be a purely material matter, but it has a very strong bearing on the spiritual aims sought. We would not take space in this little volume to give a whole chapter to the above subject had we not learned by a lifetime of experience that it is important.

The Gospel Deserves It

The gospel of Christ is the most important thing to the people of any community. People outside the church do not know this fact, but the church members do know it. The man outside frequently judges the value of the gospel by the estimate which Christians seem to put upon it. An unpainted, leaky, ill-kept churchhouse is an open proclamation of the estimate which the members put on the gospel. When an especial appeal is to be made to the man outside, he should have a visual demonstration of the value which the church people place upon the church. Freshen and clean or decorate the building. The psychological effect will penetrate the community. Here is something that tells the man outside that the members sincerely believe in the gospel.

[44]

The Best of Advertising

To reach people in a meeting we must get them to come. People like to go where things are moving forward. People like to be in on a success. Horace Greeley said, "Nothing succeeds like success." If the people of the community notice that the churchhouse is being furbished, cleaned, repaired or decorated, they feel that the church is something alive rather than something dead or dying. Their attention is attracted and their interest is aroused.

It Arouses the Interest of the Members as Well as the Outsiders

It is a universal characteristic of young and old that we are interested in a thing if we have an actual and active part in helping to make it. If all members of the church could be engaged in helping to arrange or re-arrange the churchhouse for the campaign, they would be sure to have a greater interest in the meeting. It is also true that if the man or woman outside the church can be interested to expend some of his or her energy in preparation for the meeting, either one will be interested and will very probably come to the services. A general, clean-up-and-paint party will arouse interest, advertise the enterprise and create good will. Such a move is very probably the most effective piece of advertising that can be done, especially in the smaller community.

It Creates Expectancy

One of the important things in preparing for a meeting is to create expectancy, first among the members and then among all the people of the community. Not only clean and furbish the church and the grounds, but arrange for a crowd. Place sufficient chairs to accommodate a crowd. Do not wait for a crowd to come and then prepare. Create enthusiasm by talking crowd and expecting a crowd. Let the public know you have prepared for a crowd. Arrange for abundant parking space. Let the people know that you have so arranged.

Other Equipment

Lights, songbooks, fans, furnace, baptistery, robes and every conceivable thing that has any bearing on the meeting should be checked. Poor light has a depressing effect. Add light. Cull the songbooks. Throw away or hide the disreputable old wrecks that will fall to pieces in the visitor's hands. Find some means to raise a few dollars and provide plenty of songbooks, some of which are new. Where an instrument is used, check it for performance, tuning or whatever else may be needed. In hot weather have plenty of fans which the ushers may hand out. In winter be sure the furnace will furnish heat instead of only smoke and gas. It is impossible to evangelize a crowd made stupid by smoke and gas or suffering from cold. The neglect of this one feature may defeat the whole meeting.

Have the baptistery in perfect working order, and all such matters as cloths, robes, etc., in first-class condition.

Any one of these features neglected may advertise the church as careless and indifferent, and thus kill the interest of some one whose first faint flicker of interest has been aroused. The gospel does not deserve to be obscured by dirt nor disparaged by neglect.

CHAPTER III

DISTRICTING THE TERRITORY AND TAKING A CENSUS*

"Let him know, that he which converteth the sinner from the error of his way shall save a soul from death, and shall hide a multitude of sins" (Jas. 5: 20).

Prejudice Against the Census

It is with the greatest difficulty that many ministers and church boards can be convinced of the importance of districting the territory and making an exact and complete written file of every soul within possible reach of the church. Even in the rural or semi-rural districts, this work has a number of definite advantages and values. We call attention to some of them.

Reasons for Hesitancy

The reasons for hesitancy are at least three. Probably the first is the feeling on the part of local ministers and workers that they know every one in their fields, and already know all that would be valuable to know about them. In every place where a thorough districting of territory and census taking has been used this notion has been dispelled. Local people have been literally amazed to find how little they did really know of the people and their problems, heartaches and longings, outside of the immediate membership of their own congregation. All

---

* A suggested census form, which can be printed or purchased, will be found in the appendix on page 181.

we can do here is to recommend such a move, and hope that when tried, the value will be revealed.

A second reason for hesitancy is the common and natural reticence about calling on people whom we know, to talk with them about matters religious. Calling in pairs with something definite to ask and record helps to overcome this hesitancy.

The third reason for hesitancy is the natural human tendency to avoid work. The districting requires study, i.e., headwork, and the census requires physical work and time.

Advantages of Districting

We have operated too much as a "come-to-us" institution. We forget the Great Commission says, "Go." We rejoice, and sometimes even gloat, over whatever proportion of the populace may be induced, by indirect methods, to come, but we almost ignore those people and areas which are unreached with present tactics. Our methods of reaching have, therefore, been unsystematic. The task is to reach the unreached.

The purpose of districting is to divide the territory into sections, and work each section until we know definitely that no section nor any part of a section has been overlooked. First, definitely locate the unreached.

A further purpose is that we may systematically and definitely assign the work and responsibility for a given section to some specific person or persons, and then be able to check and know when or if the work has actually been done.

Advantages of a Map

Whatever the territory, whether urban or rural, a map is of great advantage. It helps systematize, and it stares us in the face until the job is done. It helps the workers to visualize the task. It points out what has been done and what is yet to be done. It makes the work of districting and census taking much easier.

Specific Advantages of the Census

There are a number of specific advantages to the meeting if a census is taken:

(1) It discovers and lists definite prospects and gives pointedness and direct aim to the efforts of evangelist, preacher and people.

(2) It arouses interest and expectancy among the members by giving them a definite preliminary task at which at least half of the members can work.

(3) It arouses the interest of the membership in the unsaved.

(4) It makes calling easier because it gives callers a definite excuse for their calls, assigns them specific places to go and gives them something definite to say when they arrive.

(5) It is one of the most effective ways to advertise the meeting and to arouse the interest of the "outsiders."

(6) It discovers and develops workers who have not been discovered before. Young and old can be used.

How and When to Take the Census

The first move in taking a census is to secure a group of the best possible workers in the church, who can be convinced that such a move is seriously worth while. Outline the plan to them, show how it fits into the whole plan of the campaign. Exhibit the map marked into districts, and work out definite assignments of territory by sections, blocks, rural roads, or whatever. Go over the census blanks very carefully, item by item, with the workers. Give very careful instruction on how to approach people, what to do if rebuffed, how to follow up if an opening is presented and how to make note of, and turn in, interesting information not called for on the census form. The census forms should be large enough to provide room for considerable information about each member of an entire family or household. Forms can be secured from your publishing house, or can be printed by your local printer from copy of your own, but, in any case, should call for church relationships and interest of the husband, wife, and each child.

As to the time when the census should be taken, let it be far enough ahead of the campaign to allow time to complete, classify and digest the information, but not so far ahead as to lose the aroused interest.

Who Should Lead?

The workers should be made to see and feel that this is an important enterprise of the whole church and not merely a pet scheme of the minister. It is wise, therefore, to have the elders, or the board of elders and deacons, or the Bible-school superintendent and the Bible-school force made responsible for the work. The minister who attempts to do it all himself gets only a little done, compared with what a whole group can do, and he sacrifices the best means on earth for arousing and increasing the interest of the members of the congregation.

> **Five Dollars Worth of Flowers on the Hat
> and Fifty Dollars Worth on the Casket
> Can Not Take the Place of Sowing Some
> Flower Seed for Our Garden in Eternity**

CHAPTER IV

MUSIC FOR THE EVANGELISTIC CAMPAIGN

"Speaking to yourselves in psalms and hymns and spiritual songs, singing and making melody in your heart to the Lord" (Eph. 5: 19).

Why Have Music?

Why do we have music in connection with preaching, and why do we give somewhat more than the usual emphasis to the music in a revival? Is it because we unthoughtedly are merely following a custom, or is there an important place that the music fills? If so, what is that place?

Music as Worship

It is trite to say that all Christian institutions have always made music one of the forms of Christian worship, praise and adoration. We mention this first because it is the one most commonly thought of when we stop to think. Certainly, then, in the night-to-night evangelistic meeting people should be led to worship and taught to worship. Worship opens the heart. We are assembled to preach the gospel to unsaved men. Our main purpose is to present the facts and claims of the gospel, instruct the intellect and move the will, but to do this the heart must be opened, hence, the value of worship in singing as well as in prayer, Bible reading and certain phases of the preaching.

Music as Inspiration

Whether psychologists have ever offered an explanation of the fact, we do not know, but it is a recognized

[51]

fact that there is something in music that moves men, inspires men. Even the savages recognize that certain forms of music or measure make their followers ready to fight. Military music helps to lead men to war and battle. Certain forms of music soothe distracted souls. Something of music enters into the hearts of men and has an effect. The experience is practically universal. This effect, which goes into the heart and moves men, we here speak of as inspiring them. It furnishes an inner urge to thought and action. Our teaching of the truth fails unless we achieve results, i.e., get a response, a decision, action. In the choice and use of music we might well have in mind this reason for its use. This explains why one song is suitable for a funeral, another for a communion service, another fits in with prayer and another is suitable for an invitation song.

Music as Publicity

Aside from other values, music has charm. It pleases. This is not universally true, but is true for the great majority of people. Music pleases. People like it; they enjoy it because it pleases. Many people who do not have enough interest in the gospel, or concern about their souls to cause them to attend, may yet be interested in unusually good or attractive music. In this case we are legitimately using music purely for its publicity value—publicity for the gospel message which follows.

A Message in Music

While not all music has a message, some music does. This may apply either to instrumental or vocal music. The words may carry a message to the mind, or the melody itself may wield a powerful influence over the heart. It carries a heart message. It is for that reason that the conduct of the music for a good revival becomes a real art, and is so much more effective if one plans and conducts the music who understands these things.

The music conductor should be able to sense the attitude of the audience and choose the songs accordingly. A lethargic or distracted audience needs stirring music to awaken them or to call their minds together from their distractions. A frivolous audience needs music that will quiet them; a thoughtless audience needs music that will make them think and examine their lives; hence the value of a properly chosen special as a most fitting and helpful preliminary to the sermon.

Are Any Songs But the Classics Advisable?

Quite a few people have urged that all songs except the classics be ruled out in order that the people's taste for good music might be cultivated. Most of the classical hymns are of the stately, and some even of the ponderous, type. Under certain circumstances of worship they are to be much preferred, but considering all the uses for which music is to be used in revival meetings, we believe variety best serves the ends. Songs, the words of which teach un-Scriptural doctrines; songs, the tunes of which are purely jazz, or which seem to create a spirit of irreverence, and other songs of like kind, may well be avoided. Outside of this, variety is wise so that the leader may suit the song to the immediate need of the people and the evangelist. The music must appeal to the people or it has more than failed. If it does not appeal to the hearts of the people and open their hearts, it may have the opposite effect of closing their hearts and thus being hurtful instead of helpful. Keep in mind the section of the country and the community to which you are appealing.

New songs are to be used, but not overdone. People like a few new songs but, chiefly, they like to hear and to sing the old songs that they know, songs in which they can join easily and songs that stir memories.

Interesting People by Participation

We should never forget that it is a fixed and constant principle of human psychology that interest is aroused and increased by participation. The song service and the offering are the two, and about the only, parts of service in which all the people may really participate. To arouse interest in the hearts of all the people, seek to get all to sing, choose songs all can sing. It is worth much more than merely to entertain them with classics by the choir or soloist.

A Gospel Song, Sung from the Heart,

Is Often the Latch that Unlocks

The Door of the Soul

For the Gospel Message

CHAPTER V

USHERS AND USHERING

"I had rather be a doorkeeper in the house of my God, than to dwell in the tents of wickedness" (Ps. 84: 10).

The Importance of Ushers and Ushering

Ushering consists of much more indeed than merely finding seats for latecomers when the building is crowded. Ushering, properly done, can be made one of the very telling features of a meeting. If done well by carefully chosen and instructed men, the ushering may materially help to build and hold attendance, secure needed information for the evangelist and minister, assist in securing responses to the invitation, and control and prevent distractions. It is the purpose of this chapter to call attention to each of these important features. The success of a meeting depends on the smooth functioning of all parts of the organization. If every cog performs its function and fits in with all other parts, the success of the whole is much more sure. Proper ushering helps to this end.

The Head Usher

The points to be attained in a meeting are: To secure the attendance of the unchurched; make them glad they came and wish to come back the next night and every night; enable them to listen to the entire service in comfort and quietness; be in a happy and receptive frame of mind, and have the best possible opportunity

[55]

for coming forward when they are so inclined. All this, except the first item, is pretty much in the hands of the head usher.

While many men of the church may be used as ushers, including young men, the *head usher* should be one who understands all these things quite as well as does the preacher and the evangelist. Therefore, the best and most favorably known elder in the church might well be given the exceedingly important post of head usher. If he knows all the things that are dependent on him, if he understands the importance of and the details of the task, he can then definitely direct other men so that these details can be carried out. We believe this feature is as important in the small church and small community as in the larger.

The Personality of the Head Usher

Paul's description of the ideal elder (1 Tim. 3:2-7) is a good description of all that the head usher should be. He will come in closer personal contact with all who attend than any other worker in the meeting—not excepting the evangelist. New attendants are quite as likely to form their impressions of the church from the treatment which they receive under direction of the head usher as from the minister, the evangelist or the sermon. If greeted properly, treated courteously, and seated comfortably, they will be in a happy and receptive frame of mind for the service. If cared for with every tactful consideration, made to feel decidedly at home, and then sent home with as cordial a good night and invitation to come back as they received when entering the church, they will want to come again, they will come again, and the chances are they will tell their friends about the meeting and bring these friends with them when they come the next time. The head usher, therefore, should be *genial, gracious, tactful, thoughtful, "well spoken of by them that are without," "self-controlled, not easily provoked," dependable in service and have a good memory for names and faces.* Choose the head usher with care and prayer.

What the Head Usher Should Know

The head usher should be not only generally and favorably known, but he should in turn know the people. First of all, he should know which ones are already members of the congregation. Though he might not be able to know each and every one personally, yet he should know whether any one who comes in at the door is a member or is not. He should know the individuals who, though nonmembers, are nevertheless regular or occasional attendants at regular services. He should be able to note immediately some one who has come for the first time. He should also know as many people as possible, quite intimately, knowing who has been ill, who has recently had a bereavement, who has suffered a disaster or won a triumph. The more intimately he can know the people, the more valuable he is as head usher. He should also know some of the idiosyncrasies and peculiarities of some of the people, such as the hard-of-hearing, the exceedingly timid, etc. All these things are important to be kept in mind, and advantage may well be taken of the knowledge in greeting and seating the people. A final and most important thing the head usher should know is just who are active or actual prospects. This he can learn from the evangelist, the minister or the callers.

Seating and Handling the Audience

There are a number of reasons for directing the seating of an audience. We mention some of them:

(1) To prevent straggling and embarrassment. From the time an auditorium is half-filled, later comers begin to wander and hunt for suitable seats or automatically take the easiest-reached, back seat. This straggling can be entirely controlled by the usher courteously leading to a good seat which he has noted in his passing up and down the aisles.

(2) Seating prospects in advantageous seats is a point of very great importance. The minister and head usher should make use of whatever tactful means they may to induce the members of the church to be seated in the center of sections, leaving the aisle seats free; first, for those known to be immediate prospects for membership; second, for any and all strangers; and third, for latecomers. The plan should never be made public, but arranged quietly and handled quietly and tactfully.

(3) Courtesies to the attendants are important. Aside from quiet greeting, let the head usher have available a supply of songbooks to be opened at the song being sung and handed to all latecomers. Every courtesy extended helps the meeting.

It is advisable that ushers be present ahead of time, tidy the seats and floor, picking up all paper scraps, placing songbooks in racks or seats, placing flowers which may be brought, have the room well lighted and have the house generally in order. In hot weather the head usher will find it wise to have a good supply of fans. During a revival it is always well to have drinking water easily available, if conditions will at all permit.

When tracts or other literature are to be dispens
again should fall to the ushers.

Aside from all this, it pays for the head usher
keep his eyes ever open for the opportunity to extend
the courtesy of the church to strangers in ways entirely
unmentioned here.

Preventing Distractions

One distraction may wreck an entire service. The
entry of an irresponsible drunk man, a dog coming in
to seek his master, a persistently crying child, noise outside of or in some other part of the building, calls for
doctors in the audience, fire alarms, these or any one
of many other distractions can entirely wreck a service
and should be noted and handled immediately by the
head usher and his force without the minister or evangelist ever having even to take notice.

In case of a crying baby, a glass of water promptly
delivered will very frequently solve the problem. Where
it does not, a quiet offer to show the mother to a com-
fortable chair in a side room is better than to allow
hundreds of people to be irritated and distracted, and
all the value of a whole service annulled. In the case
of fire alarms, many of the members of the audience will
be uneasy, thinking their own homes may be involved.
The head usher can send some one immediately to learn
where the fire is and send a quiet note to the minister,
who can then give the information and allay the distraction afflicting the whole audience.

Help During the Invitation

If the evangelist, the minister and those who have done
calling, and who, therefore, know who the definite pros-

pects are, will point them out to the head usher, he will
also know who the definite prospects are. He can see
that they are seated next to aisles as has been suggested.
Also, the head usher, working from the back of the
room, may be in a better position than the evangelist
to take note of any one of these prospects who is under
conviction, and thus he may assist the evangelist to know
better when the invitation should be prolonged for another verse or two. Personally, we have used this plan
very successfully. Merely a raised hand of our head
usher meant, "hold on for another exhortation and verse
of invitation."

Choosing and Training Ushers

All that has been said above leads to this final paragraph. The work of the ushers, if properly done, is an
exceedingly important factor in a revival meeting. Therefore, real care ought to be given to choosing and preparing at least the head usher. Then he should secure
and *instruct* his force. The facts given in this chapter
will be of assistance to him.

Christianity can be Radiated

As Well as Preached

It Costs Little to be Courteous—

It Pays Big Dividends

CHAPTER VI

PRACTICAL SUGGESTIONS ON ADVERTISING

"Neither do men light a candle, and put it under a bushel" (Matt. 5: 15).

What Is Advertising?

Many fail to distinguish between advertising and publicity. Bills, posters, street-car signs, theater announcements, radio announcements, or display advertisements in newspapers constitute the usual means of advertising. Quite a number of novel features may be devised and added to these.

Newspaper stories, church bulletins, circular letters, etc., would be classed as publicity. We shall treat these later in Chapter VII. Here we confine the suggestions to advertising. Let it be remarked, however, that these suggestions are only illustrative. The originality, good judgment and deep interest of the one in charge of the advertising will devise or discover hundreds of means not mentioned here.

Why Advertise?

There is some prejudice against advertising the church and the gospel. When it comes to mastering the art, little has been done about it. If it is worth while to produce good sermons, it is also worth while to get the largest possible hearing for them:

(1) *Scriptural Precedent for Advertising.* There is plenty of Scriptural precedent. Under Jewish worship whole hosts of Levites blew the silver trumpets to arouse

[61]

the people to worship. Paul said, "I am made all things to all men, that I might by all means save some" (1 Cor. 9:22). Jesus fed the five thousand with loaves and fishes that He might open their ears for the message about the bread of life. The tongues of flame on Pentecost not only marked the apostles, but aroused the interest and attention of the crowd. Instances might be multiplied, bearing out the thought, "Neither do men light a candle, and put it under a bushel" (Matt. 5:15).

(2) *Another Reason for Advertising.* The church and the minister have that which the people of the community need most of all. The people do not know this fact, but here is where advertising the gospel and the church comes in. We must let them know about the gospel if we would make them to know the gospel. Preaching to empty seats makes no converts however good the sermon may be.

The Purpose in Advertising

Advertising is to attract attention to, and gain interest in, the truth. Though advertising may be, and is, used abundantly to attract attention to and gain interest for error, we may disregard that here. We are to work for the truth. Good advertising has a threefold purpose:

(1) *First, it must attract attention.* Do not try to make the advertising do the preaching. Its first requisite is to attract attention. What is there in your copy or make-up that will attract attention? Among features that count are: (a) Something new or novel, (b) something colorful, (c) something large, (d) alliterations, (e) repetitions, (f) unusual pictures, (g) something that arouses curiosity. Study every piece of advertising that attracts your attention and see what it is in it that stopped you.

[62]

(2) *Must Hold Attention.*   Second, good advertising must have something that *holds your attention* so that you read it through to the end.

(3) *Arouse a Desire to Investigate.*   The third requisite of good advertising is that it must have something that *arouses a desire to investigate* that which is advertised.   Curiosity aroused, crowd interest, actual results achieved, desire to see or hear the unusual, or a desire to have puzzling questions answered are some of the means for arousing a desire to investigate.   These are some of the things that bring people out to the meeting.

It takes *all* these three elements of attracting attention, holding the interest and arousing a desire to investigate, to make a worth-while piece of advertising.   If it fails in any one, it is a failure.   If it attracts attention merely, and does not arouse a desire to investigate, the time and money have been wasted.   Study your copy for these three things and think of it from the standpoint of the man out in the world.   If you were he, would this piece of advertising stop you, hold your attention and bring you to the meeting?

What to Advertise

Advertise only what you can deliver and then deliver what you have advertised.   If you are having crowds, advertise crowds, but unless you are dead sure of crowds, choose something else to feature.   The final test is satisfied customers.   If you advertise "the friendly church," and a new attendant meets with a cool reception, the advertising has done harm instead of good.   Stick to the strict truth in advertising for the church.   Do not advertise, "The greatest feast since Belshazzar's," and then have people come out to find you serving cold beans, weak coffee and potato salad. This is a figure which can be applied to your program and services. First, *plan and prepare something to advertise,* then tell it from the housetops. Get the crowd, deliver the goods advertised, then show them that the gospel is even more interesting. Knowles Shaw announced in the beginning of a meeting that if all the people would come out he would show them how to make a pair of shoes in a minute. That night he brought an old pair of cowhide boots, cut off the tops, slit the front and punched eyelets. Then he said, "You have come to see me make a pair of shoes in a minute, and I have. Now I am going to show you in a few more minutes how your souls can be saved for all eternity."

Definite Suggestions on Advertising

(1) *House-to-house Calling and Extending a Personal Invitation.* Actually this is advertising of the best kind possible. Call at *every* door and tell the people of the meeting. Leave the printed bill on departure.

(2) *Using Public-school Children.* Invite *all* the children of the public schools to meet you at the church. Have printed tickets handed to them at school. When they come, give them an attractive program of Christian entertainment and teaching, and then give each a piece of attractive, printed advertising to take to parents. Make the children your friends and they will be one of your best advertising mediums.

(3) *Hand Bills Must Be Attractive.* Where hand bills or dodgers are handed out, avoid the unattractive, terribly-plain, small, black-and-white dodger. It is wholly incapable of attracting attention and has been overworked years ago. It hasn't a chance unless there is something

new or catchy in the wording, or type arrangement. Remember that it takes more brains and hard work to draft an effective piece of advertising than to prepare any ordinary sermon. When prepared, secure a sufficient quantity to place one in *every* home. Avoid what has been done before. Seek something new.

(4) *Color Posters.* To get size and color make posters by hand. Printer's ink, both red and black, cut with turpentine or gasoline, and applied with a small sable brush to sheets of ordinary print paper 24-in. x 36-in., will make attractive posters. Provide boards for mounting, 24-in. x 36-in., from old lumber or boxes. Change posters regularly. Turn your fancy loose and practice. Any one can make good posters with practice.

(5) *Banners, Bumper Signs, Pennants.** Again we suggest that some one be found to do brush painting. Size and color in posters can be attained at very little cost.

(a) Get 1-in. x 2-in. pine timber, 10-ft. long. Build a frame 3-ft. x 10-ft., reinforcing the center and bracing corners and center. On this, stretch sign-painter's muslin, and with red and black printer's ink, cut with turpentine or gasoline, paint a banner to be put upon the front of the church. A suggested design appears on page 189 of the appendix.

(b) Advertising for the rear of automobile bodies or for bumpers can be made easily in the same way. Tough cardboard, fastened with wire, is suitable for bumper signs. Use sign-painter's muslin or white oilcloth for the signs to be carried on the rear of the car body. Reinforce the edges and sew on flaps for anchoring. Where oilcloth is used, use a brilliant, varnish paint.

* Suggestions for designs appear on page 189 of the appendix.

(6) *Moving Pictures as Advertising.* Moving pictures can not do the preaching, nor should they be substituted for the preaching, but if properly chosen and used in the early part of the service, they can well be used to draw the crowd for the gospel. Class them as advertising.

(7) *Theater Ads, Street-car Ads and Radio Announcements May Help.* No detailed suggestions can be valuable here, because these must be worked out locally.

The Distribution and Follow-up

Printed advertising is important enough that it deserves something more than being thrown around carelessly. Every piece should be made to count. Get each piece definitely handed to some one or some home, accompanied by a personal invitation. Therefore, it is wise for the first distribution to be made a few days before the meeting, by adults. District the territory. Assign sections to chosen *women* or *men*. Ask them to stop at each home, skipping none. Then this may be followed up on the last day before the meeting by the boys and girls hanging doorknob hangers on all the doorknobs as a final reminder. Again, district and assign. In a three weeks' meeting, follow up again at least once. Merely handing bills out at church with no systematic assignments is a decidedly ineffective and slipshod way and wastes most of the expensive printed matter.

The Best of Sermons

Can Not Bring Forth Converts

From Empty Seats

CHAPTER VII

PUBLICITY FOR THE CAMPAIGN

"The Lord gave the word: great was the company of those that published it" (Ps. 68: 11).

How Publicity Is Gained

Tons upon tons of publicity are poured out upon the public every day. We read what is said about movie actors, prize fighters, politicians, organizations, movements and cults of various kinds, and we wonder why the newspapers so avidly seek news about these, and why the editors look so glum when we take to them a story about the church. The answer is that nearly all this publicity for worldly affairs is backed by expert publicity directors who are everlastingly persistent. Even the best-known glamour girl of the movies would lose out in no time if her publicity agent should let up or prove inefficient. These agents have skill in producing stories that can be got into the papers, and persistence enough to get some of their stories over. Many of their stories are pure fakes.

How Can the Church Gain Publicity?

Whether we believe it or not, the average newspaper editor is more kindly inclined toward the local church story than he is toward this other promoted publicity, but the skilled publicity writers can produce stories which the public will read as news, while the ordinary church notice or story is so devoid of news interest that the editor can not give it much space and long remain the editor.

[67]

The only answer is for ministers and church repre-
sentatives to learn how to prepare publicity that newspapers can and will use. There are just two elements:
·One is to cultivate a sense for news interest and the other
is to learn newspaper technique in presenting the story
briefly and interestingly. We believe many editors would
be willing to give preachers free lessons in these matters.
Space does not allow us to go far into the matter here,
but a few suggestions may point the way.

Specific Suggestions

In the matter of sermon announcements, seek for something that is fitting and yet different. The sermon subject, "Elisha," has no news interest. The same sermon
given the subject, "A Plowman Turned Prophet," has
something that suggests a brief story of interest about
this plowman. The fact that your Bible school meets
at 9:30 has been reiterated *ad nauseum* and has no publicity value. The fact that you broke all records last
Sunday, or that Johnnie Jones, on his way to the First
Christian Church Sunday School, tried to run over a
Cadillac with his skooter, and broke his nose in the
attempt, has news interest around which the facts of your
service can be wound.

If a swarm of bees should settle in the belfry, how many
church folks would recognize the grand chance to make
these bees publicity agents for the church? Your ladies
made nine hundred calls for the church in a week, that
is news. With the story, weave in briefly the name, location, etc., of the church. If you raised one thousand
dollars in twenty minutes to clear the debt or the deficit,
that is news. If the church celebrated its fifth, tenth,
fiftieth or one hundredth anniversary on Sunday, that
is news. Star the main feature and briefly weave in a few

other details that will keep the church before the public. The beginning of a good revival is always news, if properly written up. The fact that the churchhouse has been cleaned and painted in readiness *for the revival* is news. The evangelist is news. The song leader is news. The total number of additions in the past ten years may be news. These are but hints. Ten thousand things lend themselves to him who has ears.

The last word is, news must be popping fresh, and the news columns are crowded. Get to the editor *promptly* and *early in the day*.

Publicity by Circular Letters

Every church ought to have a generous mailing list. This should consist of practically everybody in reach of the church. The list can be broken down into groups. One group can be made up of all parents who are not members, but whose children are in your Bible school. Another can consist of all members of all churches in the community. Any church can have a mimeograph and run off a hundred letters in an hour. In preparation for a revival send one well-worded letter to all members. Send another well-worded letter of invitation to all the parents whose children are in your school. Send other letters to other groups. Carefully word each letter to fit the group addressed.

Uncle Sam Never Refuses

To Do Church Work.

He'll Go to Every House for You

If You only Ask Him

CHAPTER VIII

CALLING: WHEN, HOW AND ON WHOM

"Go ye therefore, and teach all nations, baptizing them in the
name of the Father, and of the Son, and of the Holy Ghost"
(Matt. 28: 19).

Different Kinds of Calling

There is calling and calling. Valuable calling may be
of two kinds. The easiest is that call which is merely
friendly and gracious, but which has for its purpose to
apprise the ones called upon of the meeting and invite
them to attend. Many people can do this kind of calling.
It is valuable indeed.

A second kind of calling is that which is done with the
definite purpose of seeking an opportunity to teach, convince, convert or persuade the one called upon to obey
the gospel or to unite with the church by letter or statement. Such callers need to be equipped with Scriptural
knowledge, and need to know something of the art of
approach, of teaching and of leading to definite decision.
Not all members are equipped for such calls, but thousands
more should be. There should be training classes in every
congregation preparing groups of people for this tremendously important phase of Christian work. Such work
should be continuous and not confined merely to revival
seasons.*

Then there are the purely ineffectual and the harmful
calls. The ineffectual call is that in which the caller, be

---

* Note: The material in Part III, Section A of this book, is a short
course in doctrine, such as callers need. See also the helpful material which
is included in the appendix.

he minister or member, talks of everything and anything but the church and fails to make it plain that he has called specifically in the name of, and for, the church. Lack of nerve may be the explanation. Such calls are almost valueless. Finally there is the harmful call. Knocking, engaging in gossip, criticizing, or heated argumentation are marks of the harmful calls. May the church be delivered from such calls or callers.

Who Should Call?

Large numbers of members can be led and trained to call and do it effectually. If calling is left to the minister alone, it may have the effect of professionalism. In any case the minister can make only a fraction of the calls that should be made in preparation for the revival.

As to who should call where, that is a matter to be looked into. Nearly anyone not inclined to gossip may call at almost any door for the purely friendly, invitational call. However, when there is a more definite purpose in view, the calls ought to be carefully assigned to persons best skilled and fitted to meet the situation that is to be met in any particular case. By a preliminary call or from some other source, all possible information should be in hand about those to be called upon. Each assignment should be made to the one who is best equipped to meet the particular situation, having placed all possible information in his hands to be studied before making the call.

When to Call

If all the calling that ministers and people resolve to do were done, there would be a lot more done than is. Calls put off account for most of those not made. Therefore, we would say that the time to call is *now, this week, this evening,* or at least set aside a definite evening this week and make those calls. Most of us hesitate to call, but when we do make calls we are almost always glad and happy that we did.

From the standpoint of the one called upon, there is a warning as to the time to call. Try to choose a time which will be neither embarrassing nor too inconvenient for the one called upon. If you find you have misguessed, then make your call very brief, but arrange to call again.

On Whom Should We Call?

Remembering that we call as Christians, in the name of Christ and His church, we ought not to set a limit on the "who or where" of our calling. The nature of our approach and our objective should be determined by the situation pertaining to the one called upon, but our answer to the paragraph question is, Call *everywhere* and on *everybody.*

In preparing for a meeting, call at *every* home and tell the people about the meeting, extending a gracious invitation. Notice the word EVERY. Call not only at *every* home, but also on the storekeeper, the blacksmith, the banker, the gas-station attendant, the manufacturer, the shut-in, the good people, the bad people, and all. You are not calling for yourself or in your own name, but for Christ and in His name.

Why Should We Call?

There are some tremendous reasons as to why we should call. The first is that Christ commanded it. He said, "Go ye." We have builded a churchhouse and say, "Come." Christ said, "Go." That "Go ye" is directed to every Christian and it means *go.*

Second, it is a fact that New Testament precedent sets the example for going to the people. We claim to be desirous of restoring the New Testament church. Note that when the members of that first church in Jerusalem were scattered to the four quarters of the earth, they went everywhere preaching the Word. Not only the apostles like Peter and Paul, the deacons like Philip and Stephen, but the *disciples* did this. These, then, are the Scriptural reasons.

There is also a very practical reason. After nearly two thousand years, less than one-third of the human race has ever even heard of Christ. In America, more than half the population, that is to say, sixty-four millions out of one hundred twenty-seven millions of the people, make no pretense at being Christian. Seventeen millions of American boys and girls of school age, that is exactly half, are growing up with no semblance of Christian teaching or training. Until and unless the whole body of Christians develops a conscience on this matter, the condition will remain the same.

Two final reasons for calling are: First, if we call generously there are some who will be turned to Christ and be saved who otherwise would not. There is a reward to the worker. The second reason is that here is one of the best ways on earth to help the caller to grow in grace and knowledge of the truth.

How to Call

Perhaps it would take a whole volume to go into the details of, "How to Call." We can but make one or two pointed suggestions here. The "How to Call" is important. Most Christians refuse to call, or hesitate to call, or procrastinate about calling because they feel that they do not know how. They are embarrassed because they do not know how to approach strangers, what to say first and what to say next. They do not know how to direct conversation so that it will lead directly to the point which is the purpose of the call. Knowing that they do not know how, they hesitate.

Effectual calling can be learned by any sincere and earnest Christian. But like many other things, such as playing the piano or fixing a radio, it has to be learned. In the above and all other cases it takes *information* and *practice*. From the minister or a good book, get all the information possible. A recent and inexpensive book, entitled "Personal Evangelism," deals directly with the problem of "How to Call." The final way then is, as in any other thing, practice. Call and call and call, checking your errors and correcting your mistakes, adding to your knowledge and profiting by your experience. Get pleasure out of learning it as a fine art and a most needed service. When we Christians take this "Go ye" seriously, great revivals will be reported from every quarter and in every congregation. Tens of thousands will be turned to the Lord, and the church of the Lord will begin to come into its own.

"To Everything There is a Season."
There's Even a Time for Knocking,
Provided It Consists of Knocking
on Doors in the Name of Christ

CHAPTER IX

PREPARATORY DOCTRINAL TEACHING

"Preach the word" (2 Tim. 4: 2).

We Must Sow If We Would Reap

Reaping appeals to most people. The months of patient sowing are not so appealing. In a former chapter we have suggested that the evangelist for the next evangelistic campaign be decided upon and secured almost a year ahead of time. If this is done and the general date determined, many other things may be done to prepare for the meeting. Among these is a definite program of doctrinal teaching, preaching and tract distribution. We too often depend on the evangelist or the minister-evangelist to do all the indoctrinating as well as convincing, convicting and reaching of the unsaved. The relatively short period of a revival is too brief to permit one man to do all these things effectively for all the people reached. The Scriptural example is "teach, baptize, teach" (see Matt. 28: 19, 20). We should indoctrinate, baptize, indoctrinate. Teach all the New Testament first principles possible in preparation for decision, then form a definite program of doctrinal instruction by preaching and by teaching in the Bible school or special class, for new converts after the meeting. (This latter subject is treated in Part IV of this book.)

Preliminary Teaching

In every class in the Bible school above the Primary Department, it is advisable to add definitely doctrinal

[75]

teaching in addition to the regular lessons for eight or ten weeks before the evangelistic campaign. The materials contained in Part III, Section A, of this book are included as a suggestion and help to this end.

The minister and the Bible-school superintendent should jointly lay out a program and prepare all teachers to enter into a plan which covers the entire school above the Primary Department. There are many inexpensive helps, Bible drills and supplementary tracts and booklets that can be used for this purpose. Such a program, systematically carried out for some months before the meeting, will mean a sowing that will almost guarantee an abundant harvest when the reaping time comes.

A further suggestion is that exhibits of doctrinal-teaching drills by various classes be made a feature of the opening exercises in Bible school at frequent intervals. Such a program not only indoctrinates the children who participate, but also all who hear. (Illustrated, page 184.)

Another valuable way to implant the primary doctrines of the New Testament is to draw up a catechetical list of questions and answers on the gospel plan of salvation and use it as a feature of the opening exercises in the whole school, or in all departments regularly or at frequent intervals. Part III, Section B, of this book is an illustration of how to prepare and use this feature. (Page 165.)

Doctrinal Preaching in Preparation for the Meeting

There are at least three purposes in doctrinal preaching prior to and in preparation for the revival or harvest time.

First, the members of the church need to be revived, renewed, re-inspired and re-fired with the simple terms of the gospel which one day reached and moved them. Second, the members need to be reviewed and refreshed in the simple gospel teaching, that they may be ready and inclined to help interest and teach others when the campaign is on. Third, doctrinal preaching prepares the unreached attendant for definite decision during the revival, if not before.

What Is Doctrinal Preaching?

In one sense, any preaching that clearly imparts any of the New Testament teaching is doctrinal preaching. However, such a conception is too broad to be entirely practical in sermons definitely planned to prepare for the evangelistic meeting. That meeting is planned for the unreached, the untaught, the uninterested and even the indifferent. They must be planned for as unborn children. Milk, not meat, is in order. First principles plainly presented must be in the foreground. It is this preaching of basic, plain, first principles that is needed when sowing for the future reaping. New subjects, new heads, new dresses may be used for the sermons, but the old themes must be used to be effective. First principles are yet first principles whatever our personal attitude may be. The first of first principles is "faith." If ever there was a time when the world needed *faith* more than now we can not conceive when it was. "Repentance" is still of prime importance, and likewise every item of what has been known as "first principles."

The Bread of Life, After All,

Was Intended for Sheep and Lambs

Rather Than for Giraffes

CHAPTER X

FINANCING THE CAMPAIGN

"For where your treasure is, there will your heart be also" (Luke 12: 34).

Financial Problem Need Never Prevent a Meeting

While we shall say later, that it is better to leave the actual financing of a meeting until the meeting is under way, we discuss the matter at this time under the head of "Preparing the Field for the Campaign," for two reasons.

The first of these reasons is, that the financial phase always comes into the forefront in the board meetings, when the matter of planning for a proposed meeting is under discussion, and, too often, the attitude is taken, "It is with the greatest difficulty that we can pay our current expense bills, and it would be out of the question to pay for a revival meeting." It is the purpose of this chapter to show that a properly planned and conducted meeting, not only pays for itself, but actually makes it easier to raise the current-expense budget.

The second reason for discussing the matter at this point is directly the opposite of the first. There are some churches and ministers who are careless about, or inclined to disregard, the financial end of the meeting. What we wish to say here is, that though in nearly every case it is better to leave the *actual financing* until the meeting is under way, yet the *definite plans* for the financing, a carefully estimated budget, and an understanding as to how, when and by whom it shall be raised, should be most certainly determined in the preliminary planning. Unpaid bills of the church are a serious hindrance to the church and the meeting. Farther on we give the reasons why we believe the actual raising of funds should be only planned but not put in action until the meeting is under way. The thing to be kept in mind here is that revival financing is the easiest of all financing, and that a good revival is a *financial asset* to the church *rather than a liability*.

Plans Must Be Determined by Local Conditions and by the Evangelist

Before we attempt to make specific suggestions about plans for financing, it should be made plain that there is no one plan suited to all places and times. Some congregations have very definitely fixed plans which they have used successfully for years, and a change in plan might not be advisable. Again, among the evangelists secured there will be found many plans, some one of which it might be advisable to try.

In general, however, it is usually *much more advisable* for the church itself to assume and control the financing through its own board and minister, than to turn a mere temporary leader loose to raise all he can in any way he can. Most successful evangelists are experts in raising money and there is no reason why their ability should not be used, but it should be as a carefully planned part of the work of the financial committee for the meeting.

In planning use horse sense. Evangelistic meetings can be conducted at a cost all the way from a few dollars up to thousands. Plan a meeting the costs of which are within reason and it can be financed.

Reasons for Deferring Actual Financing

There are a number of reasons, which we believe to be good ones, for making the raising of the costs of the meeting a part of the meeting after it is under way. While it may be necessary to raise a limited amount in cash to take care of early expenses, such as the first advertising bills, the evangelist's traveling expense, etc., the securing of the main part of the costs can well be deferred. We do not pretend to give these reasons in any order as to their importance.

(1) *Put early effort into making the meeting succeed.* If the minister and board have faith in themselves, in their evangelist, in their plans and in the people, they can then cease worrying about finances, and the evangelist and whole congregation can throw their entire strength and effort toward making the meeting succeed. This applies up to about the middle of the meeting. Merely take the offering *each* night, explain what it is for and let it go at that. There is a good psychological reason, which we shall give later, for taking the offering. Take it. Hold it separate. Do not allow a penny of it to be spent for any other purpose than the costs of the meeting.

(2) *Wait for the larger attendance and warmer interest.* If all efforts are bent on preaching, singing, calling and personal work, the meeting will be at a good point of interest near the middle of the time allotted for it. The attendance will be better than at regular services, the interest and spirit of the members will be high, many others than regular attendants will be attending. The raising of such money as needed will be many times easier, and participated in by many more people than if presented cold to only those who usually bear the brunt of all financing.

(3) *Give every one the benefit of helping.* Where all provision is made for the financing before the meeting starts, it is almost certain that the money will be contributed by only a few. They have deprived all the rest of the interest that comes from having a part in it. Any lukewarm member, or any outsider who comes to the meeting and puts a dime into the offering will have a dime's worth of interest in the meeting. We are all more interested in that which we help to pay for, even though our contribution may be small. The outsider who puts in a dime has invested. That investment may arouse the first beginnings of an interest that will lead him to come again, hear and obey the gospel and become a substantial member of the church. Give everybody a chance. Take an offering every night.

If one or two generous brethren would and should assume and pay all the bills of the meeting, it would be next to disastrous to the meeting. As was said in a former chapter, "participation creates interest." We need the interest of as nearly everybody as possible. Therefore, give the largest possible number the chance to participate. This can operate fully only when the meeting has progressed to full attendance.

The singing and the giving are the only two features in which literally all can participate. Therefore, defer the main raising of funds until the interest is aroused and the largest possible number of members and outsiders are attending.

In a three-week meeting, set aside a definite, brief period in the opening services on about the second Sunday night of the meeting, present the matter plainly, briefly and frankly. State as nearly as possible what the total cost is, and what the main items of cost consist of. State what has come in to date in miscellaneous offerings

[81]

and a fair estimate of the amount to be counted on in the remaining loose offerings. Then in twenty minutes enough money can be raised in cash and seven-day pledges to clear all costs, and frequently enough to give a New Testament to each new member, pay for the refreshments to be served at a reception for the new members and possibly turn a balance into the current-expense treasury. The people are happy over the success to date, they are delighted over those who have come, their interest is keen, they know what they are paying for and they are, therefore, in a giving mood. This is but one plan. It is suited to a three or four weeks' meeting where there is an employed evangelist. This method, where used, actually helps the meeting. People who give are more inclined to come again, they are more inclined to work, the unchurched are more likely to obey the gospel.

Various Plans of Financing Meetings

We mention a number of the usual plans for raising the costs of meetings. No one is perfect, and no one fits all places, times or groups.

(1) *Pre-campaign cash plan.* This is a plan by which the costs are estimated and the full budget raised in cash or pledges before the meeting begins. This can be done in some places, but has the serious defects which we have discussed above.

(2) *The underwriting plan.* In this case the whole estimated cost is raised in conditonal pledges, such that the total equals the total cost. Then during the meeting miscellaneous offerings are taken. These are subtracted from the total cost, and the balance needed is prorated among those who gave underwriting pledges.

(3) *The plan where all participate.* This plan is the one explained at length above and has the advantages

pointed out. It is capable of many variations, which may be suggested by the minister or the evangelist.

(4) *The so-called freewill-offering plan.* This plan provides that the evangelist is to come, hold the meeting, be responsible for the money-raising, raise all he can and take what he gets. This plan is so loose and unbusinesslike that it lends itself to innumerable abuses, misunderstanding and long-standing harm to the whole cause of evangelism. What we say here has in mind the church which is strong enough to employ an evangelist, and which is using an employed evangelist dependent on the income from his evangelism for his living. The criticism does not apply to meetings wholly or partly donated to closed or weaker churches by pastors or other congregations. In such cases the strictly freewill-offering plan is about the only feasible one.

Advantages and Disadvantages of the Freewill-offering Plan

One of the advantages of the freewill-offering plan is that it is much easier to induce many congregations to accept such a plan. Their lethargy, or their lack of faith, or their desire to get something for as nearly nothing as possible leads many congregations to insist on this plan. Knowing their own penuriousness they are willing to assume neither obligation nor responsibility. They are sure the evangelist will get much less than the legitimate weekly, straight salary which he asks, and are content thus to play unfair with the laborer. To overcome this unfair attitude the evangelist is compelled to divert evangelizing power to money-raising. Such blame as reverts to the money-raiser falls on the head of the evangelist and therefore operates against the meeting.

[83]

To top it all off, if the evangelist by chance should be an exploiter, he is in position to press and promote the matter to ends that are indeed profitable to him and hurtful to the church for years to come. In some such cases, the promised freewill-offering becomes a highly promoted, high-pressure money-raising. We advise this plan, if no better can be arrived at. But a definitely agreed-upon, businesslike arrangement in which the congregation participates in the planning, raising and handling of the fund is much less liable to reveal serious disadvantages. Largely, it is the congregations that are responsible for this plan.

Adopt Some Plan and Proceed

Naturally, we can not go into detail as to all the plans. There are almost as many variations in plans as there are evangelists. We only urge that this matter be worked out, with understanding, by the evangelist and a representative of the congregation, the two working together as Christians, both with the one aim of saving souls kept in the foreground. Take advantage of all the wisdom and experience of the evangelist in this matter, make use of his ability, but work with him and plan that he work with you as the meeting proceeds. Adopt some plan and go ahead. If a mistake is made, do not sour on evangelists and evangelism. Locate the source of the mistake and refrain from making such a mistake again rather than refraining from evangelism henceforth, as some do.

Meetings that Require Little or No Financing

Most of what has been said has applied to the meeting planned for a going congregation, large or small, employing a regular evangelist. In order that we may make clear that the financing problem does not stand in the way of any and every congregation having a revival each year, we mention some of the plans where little or no finance problem is involved.

(1) *For the very small, weak, poor or closed church.* There is the possibility of securing the near-by minister of a stronger, sister church to conduct a donated or volunteer meeting. In this case his home congregation agrees to continue his weekly salary for the time. The freewill offerings easily care for his added expenses, for the small, local expenses and frequently a bit over to recompense the minister for his added labor. Such a meeting is known as a "Contributed," "Volunteer," "Big Brother," or "Group Evangelism" meeting. Hundreds of our ministers now hold such meetings each year.

(2) *Vacation meetings.* Many ministers of larger churches, men of evangelistic ability, are willing to conduct meetings during their vacations on very reasonable terms.

(3) *Exchange meetings.* In many of the churches, large and small, the ministers hold exchange meetings, cutting the costs largely to mere personal expenses aside from local costs of printing, etc.

(4) *Lay evangelists.* As we have checked the records of our brotherhood, we find that there are a surprising number of business-men preachers who, either singly or in teams, conduct many successful revivals each year for expenses or little more.

(5) *The home-force meeting.* Little need be said as to financing the home-force meeting, except that if the local minister serves as evangelist he works at some disadvantage and should have the more generous backing

of his members in work, publicity, advertising and loyalty than might be given to any other evangelist.

The conclusion of the whole matter of this chapter is that every congregation can have a revival each year. The financial problem can always be solved.

How Many People are in the Poorhouse
Because of What They Gave to the Lord?
How Many are There Because
of What They Gave to the Devil?

PREPARING THE MEMBERSHIP FOR THE CAMPAIGN, IN SPIRITUALITY, INTEREST, INCENTIVE AND EXPECTANCY

"Prepare ye the way of the Lord, make his paths straight" (Matt. 3: 3).

It Takes a Whole Church to Conduct a Successful Meeting

Our most outstanding evangelists have always insisted that successful leadership in evangelism consists of the art or ability to get everybody to work. The idea has prevailed, however, quite widely, that it is the evangelist who holds the meeting. It certainly needs no argument to prove that if the minister is intensely interested and earnest, if every elder is actively and earnestly interested, if the Bible-school officers and teachers are actively interested, and, finally, if the great body of the membership can be aroused to a real interest, a successful meeting is half held and the results are all but assured. Therefore, among the early prepa-

[87]

rations there is nothing more important than a well-laid program calculated to accomplish these very ends.

Spirituality of the Working Membership

There are varying views of what constitutes spirituality, but at least we can all agree that noticeable features of it are: An earnest desire to clean up life in the matters of act, word and thought; a greater degree of interest in, and loyalty and devotion to, the church; and a noticeably deeper desire to see Christ glorified, the church triumphant and the lost saved.

There is, therefore, much more to spirituality than the mere assumption of a superior piety and a critical attitude toward the weaker brother. Christ's spirituality burned brightest and showed clearest in His wholly unselfish and sympathetic interest in others. The promotion of a sincere interest in others is one of the best means to an increased spirituality among the working members. This is especially true provided it is accompanied by an urgency to make the lives of the Christians more fitting examples, and less frequently stumbling-blocks to others.

Removing a Stumblingblock

One of the most serious hindrances to a successful reaching of the unsaved is the accumulated load of backslidden, indifferent, nonparticipating and sometimes openly sinful, members. What can be done to alleviate this condition?

The aim should be the same; that is, to arouse or create a greater spirituality, interest and incentive. But, as these members do not attend, they can not be reached by any program confined to the churchhouse.

One of our most successful evangelistic ministers from Des Moines, Ia., has furnished this suggestion: "Go over the church roll carefully and prayerfully and divide the inactive list into age groups, such as teen-age, the twenties, thirties, etc. Then call the leaders of all Sunday-school classes. Assign the names to the proper group leaders to be reached by them and their pupils. List the classes on a blackboard and after each class set down the number of inactive members assigned to them. At times call the leaders together for definite reports and check-up. Guide, counsel and encourage, for many weeks of persistent work may be needed. Make note of every success.

"Two or three things will be accomplished: The sick, the poor and the discouraged nonattendants will be discovered. Many will be restored to attendance, all will be helped some, and the coming revival will be well advertised."

Activity Begets Interest and Spirituality

As has been said before, spirituality and incentive grow out of interest. Interest is best aroused and increased by participation, i. e., by actual co-operation in work. Many of the preparatory means suggested in former chapters are, therefore, well suited to achieve these ends. Not only the work suggested in the preceding paragraph is conducive to an increased spirituality and interest, but all participation, such as setting the building in order, taking the census, building up the Bible school in preparation for the meeting, and any and all other activities that set the largest possible number actually at work for the meeting. Even the indifferent ofttimes show life if asked to do a definite task.

[89]

Prayer a Means Toward Spirituality, Interest and Incentive

Many would reverse the order of this paragraph and the one preceding. Personally, we have found that it is easier to get the average church member to do a definitely assigned piece of work and thus arouse an interest which in turn makes it easier to interest him in the prayer life. However that may be, prayer is an indispensable means to spirituality. A definite program to promote grace and prayer in all the homes is a good first move. Let every teacher in the Bible school, in all classes from kindergarten to adult, be encouraged to put on a program of prayer *and of teaching her pupils how to pray*. Encouragement may well be given to a wider participation of the membership in the prayers during the regular services. When all this is done, it will probably be found much easier to revive and enlarge the midweek prayer meeting. Add to this the circle of neighborhood cottage prayer meetings, and a real contribution to prayer life and to the meeting has been made. The cottage prayer meeting is discussed more in detail in a following chapter.

Doctrinal Preaching and Spirituality

The gospel is the power of God unto salvation. Salvation consists of more than the mere steps into Christ. Faithfulness, perseverance, growth in grace and knowledge of the truth, and service for Christ are all integral parts of salvation. The gospel is the power all along the line. There is nothing so valuable toward rekindling the fires of interest, incentive and a desire to persevere, as that same gospel that one time touched our hearts and led us to Christ. Gospel preaching, rather than mere delivery of addresses on various themes political, social and economic, is that which will fire, inspire and spiritualize. "Preach the Word." Teach the Word in all the teaching agencies of the church. Equip all members to teach others, and their own incentive and spirituality will be enhanced.

Creating Expectancy

Along with all our other restoring of the New Testament church, confidence in the *power of the gospel* is much needed to be restored. In a former chapter we said: "Prepare for a crowd, expect a crowd and the chances are you will have a crowd." Expect additions. Have confidence enough to insist that the baptistery be in readiness; ask the women to prepare baptismal robes; train one deacon and one deaconess to assist at baptisms; put a few, new blank sheets in your rollbook. If the minister, as leader, lacks confident expectancy, he can not possibly create it in the membership. Unless such is created in the membership, one of the greatest helps to a successful revival has been lost. An illustration is found in a story of Evangelist Knowles Shaw. He went into a new community to do preaching in the schoolhouse. First, however, he borrowed a dirt shovel and went to the creek and began damming it up. Naturally a crowd gathered. They asked him what he was doing. He replied that he was making a place to baptize people. They asked him whom he expected to baptize, and he merely replied, "You people," and went on shoveling dirt. The outcome was that he did baptize many of them and started a church.

Knowing What Is Done in Other Places

One of the finest ways to create interest and expectancy for the coming revival is to induce the largest possible number of people to read the telegrams and news reports every week, which tell of the meetings going on in other places and the victories that are being won. Our national church journals carry this news from every quarter of the country every week. Many state church papers carry much of such news for the state. Choice and inspiring bits of evangelistic news can be copied in the church bulletins for weeks before the meeting begins. Every one who can be induced to read this news will be found to have an increasing interest in the home campaign.

A Final Means

One of the final means for creating expectancy, not only among the membership, but throughout the community, is a generous, widespread and thorough program of advertising and publicity. This includes: All programs of calling; good, printed advertising, and publicity in circular letters, church bulletins and newspapers. One announcement is not enough. Find ways to keep the church and the meeting in the mind of the public for weeks or even months before the meeting begins. Then intensify just before the beginning. Keep it up during the meeting.

Using All Means

No *one* of the above suggestions will accomplish the purpose. Put them *all* to work, and then add a number of means which you and your members will think of as you plan. You can then confidently expect a noticeable increase in spirituality, interest, incentive and expectancy.

CHAPTER II

PLANNING AND CONDUCTING COTTAGE PRAYER MEETINGS

"The effectual fervent prayer of a righteous man availeth much" (Jas. 5: 16).

Not a Necessity, But a Valuable Help

The cottage prayer meeting is not an absolute necessity, but may be made a most helpful asset. This, however, depends almost entirely on how the meetings are planned, promoted and conducted. Merely going through the motions of cottage prayer meetings may only use up good energy, wear down the interest of good members and achieve little or nothing definitely worth while. An unplanned, undirected and directionless program is not conducive to interest, enthusiasm or spiritual growth.

What Is a Cottage Prayer Meeting?

A "cottage prayer meeting" can be conducted in a mansion, an apartment or a cottage; that is to say, in a home. It could more fittingly be described as a *"neighborhood* prayer meeting." Such a meeting has a number of purposes, the first of which is to bring the prayer service of the church into more intimate contact with the church homes and closer to many of the unreached in the various neighborhoods. Other purposes would be: To multiply the number of prayer meetings, increase the number interested in promoting them and, in a sense, carry out the "Go ye" motive of the gospel rather than merely the "come" motive.

Planning the Meetings

We have said that the value of these meetings depends on planning, promotion and conduct. Anything that is worth doing at all is worth doing well. The program of a cottage prayer meeting, while simple, ought to be as carefully planned as any service of the church. Definite topic to be studied or followed, choice of Scriptures, choice of songs, provision for songbooks and Testaments and careful preparation by the leader are indispensable to a resultful cottage prayer meeting. In preparation for a revival meeting, the choice of topics, Scriptures and songs for the prayer meeting should be in keeping with the fact that evangelism is in the air. Special musical features, suitable readings or special Bible teachings may be used to advantage. Where desired, a Christian social half-hour and light refreshments may be added. By some means the spirit of brotherhood, friendliness and warmth must be achieved.

Promotion of Cottage Prayer Meetings

The determination to hold cottage prayer meetings may well originate with the minister, but the whole plan and program ought to be sponsored by and plans laid by and in the whole board or at least in the board of elders. There are many plans of promotion. We suggest but one. Of course, it is expected that announcements, bulletin notices and such like will be used. Also, it is much wiser to plan comprehensively, i. e., for the whole series rather than one meeting at a time.

The following plan has been successfully used. Ask for invitations from a large number of homes. Choose homes which will locate the meetings in each section, ward or neighborhood. Appoint the lady of each home chosen as hostess (not leader). Instruct her that she is to be wholly responsible for the *attendance* at this *one* meeting. Place in her hands the list of all members in her territory, giving addresses and phone numbers. Instruct her to invite, by postal or telephone, each of these and, in addition, as many as she can of her neighbors who are not members. This latter is quite important in preparing for a revival. Back this hostess up, assist her and check up on progress. Give her such help or helpers as she may need. Assure her that she will be responsible for this one meeting only, but that you are looking to her to do her utmost for this one. This plan has worked well in many places.

The Program

The program of a cottage prayer meeting preliminary to a revival can well be made definitely evangelistic. Any message of the minister should be short, not over fifteen minutes, but if made up of carefully prepared, clear-cut and condensed gospel teaching, followed by a suitable invitation song, three things may be accomplished. First, the members will be re-taught, refreshed, re-inspired and re-equipped. Second, the unchurched will receive needed teaching, which may bear fruit later. Third, decisions for Christ may be brought about, and this in itself will only create greater interest in the coming revival.

If this suggestion be added to those in the paragraph on planning, little more need be said as to program.

Conduct of the Meeting

While there is value in training as many as possible to conduct meetings by actually appointing them to conduct, yet we suggest that inasmuch as these cottage meetings are an important feature in a very important campaign of the year, only skilled conductors be appointed. With a good and successful hostess securing worth-while attendance, and with a carefully planned program, the effect of the prayer meeting may yet be annulled by a poor conductor. This, however, is a matter which can be worked out only locally.

Conserve the Results and Carry Through

Every good achieved should be conserved. Every prospect discovered should be card-filed and followed up. Watch to discover and encourage every indication of new leadership ability. Note and commend every piece of work well done by the hostess or others. Cultivate and follow up each new acquaintance made. Gather addresses of all new acquaintances for the mailing list.

A Plan That Was Used

One of our most aggressive and efficient elders, who is also the Bible-school superintendent in his church, submitted the following plan, which was used most successfully in preparation for their last revival: "Starting weeks before the meeting begins, we have four cottage prayer meetings each week in convenient places in town in the homes of the members, on Monday, Tuesday, Thursday and Friday nights. We center all of our energy at the church on Wednesday nights. This we do for three weeks. The fourth week, on Monday and Tuesday nights, we have ten prayer meetings each night, closing our prayer meetings on Wednesday night in the church with an all-night prayer meeting starting at 6:00 p. m. and closing at 6:00 a. m. We have a new leader to come on each half hour of the night, the leader being responsible for his group to attend. In our meeting this summer our group did not fall below

[96]

seventeen at any time of the night, and ran as high as sixty.

"Thus we have brought a prayer meeting in reach of every member. In all of these prayer meetings the whole theme is the revival. This summer we wrote to the leaders in all of the churches in a radius of twenty-five miles, about twenty in number, asking them to have a special prayer meeting, praying for the success of our meeting, the same Wednesday night that we had our all-night prayer meeting."

The Real Apostles' Creed

of a Real Apostle [Peter]

Reads as Follows: "Thou Art

the Christ, the Son of the Living God."

CHAPTER III

SECURING AND USING PROSPECT AND PRAYER LISTS

"Where there is no vision, the people perish" (Prov. 29: 18).

Sight the Gun Before Pulling the Trigger

Evangelism is rightly builded on hope and confident expectation, but this is not to be done to the neglect of definite and sensible planning. Hoping to reach one hundred additions may prove vain indeed. Knowing exactly where there are one hundred people that may possibly be reached, knowing who they are and working directly for that particular one hundred, will in all probability reach fifty of them and with them another fifty not previously thought of. Every person reached opens the way to another.

We arrived on a field early one Monday morning to begin a three weeks' meeting that night. The church was in a small rural village. We asked the minister how many people we might expect to reach. We were delighted and surprised to hear him say, "We ought to reach one hundred." We began to ask questions to find who and where this hundred were to be found. We asked about the young people, and he said that all who were old enough were in the church. Then we inquired about the names of unchurched people whom he hoped to reach. After long questioning, he could mention only three individuals, and all these three were gospel-hardened sinners who had been worked upon for years. As a result, it took much of the time of the meeting actually to locate a prospect list.

[98]

Contact Must Be Established

The gospel is the power of God. Likewise, an engine is the power of a threshing machine, but it takes a connecting belt to get the power to the right place, turn the wheels and thresh out the grain. Dynamite has power, but it can be shot off in the air and result only in noise. To do the work, it must be placed under that which is to be moved.

Plans for Locating Prospects

(1) *Prospect cards.* Prepare cards (3 x 5) on which these words are printed: "Following and on reverse side are names and addresses of people whom I hope to see won during the campaign. I will work and pray for these that they may be won." Leave space for addresses and phone numbers under each dotted line used for a name. Ask all the church members to remain for a short after-meeting following some regular service prior to the revival. After a very brief explanation and prayer, hand one or two cards to each member. Urge and encourage each to write down a number of names, assuring them that the information will be kept confidential, if they so request. Then have each one to sign his or her own name at the top of the card. These cards can be made so that the list is in duplicate, and the one filling the card can keep his copy as a prayer list, as a reminder and as a means of checking off those reached, when reached.*

(2) *Using the teachers.* Meet with Bible-school teachers, including *all* from kindergarten to adult groups. In large schools they can be called by departments. There are things to be accomplished here. Insist that every teacher furnish a list of any and all pupils enrolled, who are not

---

* Sample copy of such a card appears on page 182 in the appendix of this book.

members of the congregation. Beginners and Primaries are excepted. Then ask all teachers, *including* those of the Beginners and Primary Departments, to furnish a list of all parents of their pupils, who are not members of the congregation. If they do not have the information, urge them to secure it by calling, or by inquiry, and furnish it at the earliest possible time. The third thing is to furnish all teachers lists of prospects secured from other sources and ask them to contact them for their Bible-school classes. It is important that every bit of helpful information possible about each prospect be noted down for the guidance of possible callers later.

(3) *Class roll cards.* If 3 x 5 cards are used for class roll cards, there will be found much room for information. Not only the pupil's name, address, telephone number, birthday and class assignment can be noted, but the facts as to the pupil's church relationship and the names and church relationships of both parents. This gives a most valuable and fruitful prospect list for the revival.

(4) *Lists collected by callers.* In distributing advertising, we have urged that it be systematically handed in at *every* home, bar none. We have also suggested that this printed matter be not merely tossed at people, but that preferably the ladies of the church make at least the first round, knock at each door and extend a personal invitation to the meeting and then leave the piece of printed matter. A word of introduction and explanation as to what church they represent will many, many times bring a response that reveals an active prospect. Make written note at once and turn it in.

(5) *Using new members.* As soon as any new members are reached, go to them at once and ask them to cite you to prospects. Here is one of the most fertile sources. Each new person won will reveal the way to another.

3545

(6) *The census.* We have mentioned this plan last because it is discussed at length in Section A, page 47. We only add here that this is the one thoroughgoing method, but to be valuable to your congregation should be done by your congregation rather than to depend on fragmentary information culled from a general or interchurch census.

Using the Information

It should be quite unnecessary to say that none of the above has much value unless actively followed up and worked. The earlier in the meeting every lead can be followed, the better. It is not only legitimate but advisable to follow up the most favorable prospects first. If the most promising prospects can be reached early in the meeting, their coming will make the approach to the less promising prospects easier.

Where there are many prospects, as there should be in any community except the smallest, divide the prospects among the members of a well-chosen calling committee. Cover the ground promptly. Have callers *write down every* bit of information gained, as well as the result of the call in each case. Never depend on memory. Follow up, change callers. Send the minister and evangelist in where others fail and where the situation seems fertile. Follow every lead, investigate every prospect. Read again the Master's story of the great feast.

A Sermon of Any Length is Far Too Long

for Some People Who Must Hurry Home

to Listen to the Radio

CHAPTER IV

THE MINISTER'S WORK IN ORGANIZATION OF THE FORCES AND ASSIGNMENT OF TASKS

"Do the work of an evangelist, make full proof of thy ministry" (2 Tim. 4: 5).

The Minister as We Know Him

While by strict New Testament precedent the minister is primarily a preacher of the Word, that is to say, an evangelist, yet as we operate today we look upon our ministers as the general leaders in all the enterprises of the congregation, inspiring, training, teaching, planning, leading and directing. Certainly they are thus legitimately employed in evangelism if they can so lead and direct that they can make evangelists of all of us, which is, again, a New Testament ideal. It is a fact that if the minister does not lead and direct, the rest of us make little progress in evangelizing the unevangelized.

Organizing the Forces

There are some wrong notions of organization. Merely to announce the names of a lot of people on committees is far from organizing. Merely to divide the names of the members into groups, calling one group the "evangelistic committee"; another, the "advertising committee"; another, the "finance committee," etc., is not organization at all.

A working organization begins with a study of what is to be done. Break this down into definite and specific tasks. Do this with the help of as many workers as possi-

[102]

ble so that all know what is to be done and the various details of the task. Then, with their help and suggestions, pick the best suited man or woman in the whole congregation as the head of a group or committee for each division or specific part of the work. With these heads, help to choose other helpers on each committee. Then make it plain that each group will be absolutely depended upon to carry through the work assigned, and that if any leader fails, the work of all is liable to fail. This is actual organization.

If the minister tries to do it all, the rest are willing to have him do it, but nine-tenths of the power of the whole church is lost. Let the minister first divide and assign the work as suggested and then let him also do his part, assisting, guiding and encouraging all along the line. Let him make note of how each and every committee is progressing and call the heads of committees for a check-up and report.

Making Assignments Plain

Most church members, even many of the apparently indifferent, are willing to work if given something definite and specific to do that they can do. Too often they are urged to "Help work for the Lord," without any idea of what is to be done, what they could do, or when, where or how to do it. If asked by the minister to do a specific thing, they feel complimented by being asked, and pleased at being trusted. Their interest is increased by the fact of their being put to work. Here, then, is the great task for the minister; to keep in mind all the multiplied details of things that should be done to make the meeting a success, and to separate these into definite tasks, and get each task assigned to the most suitable person to carry out that piece of work. If the suggestions made in this book are carried out, there is a work for all, including officers, teachers, men, women and even the boys and girls. The only reason more of them do not do more is that they have not been given definite things to do.

Enough for the Minister to Do

If the minister keeps in active and co-operative touch with church-repair committee, census committee, prayer-meeting committee, prospect-finding committee, advertising and publicity committee; confers and plans with the Bible-school superintendent and teachers; works with his board of elders; does his share of the calling; guides in the doctrinal teaching and does doctrinal preaching in preparation for the meeting, and inspires all the rest to work, he will have quite enough to do. All these things are important and, if he can do these things, much more will be accomplished than if he makes of himself the one and only pack horse for the whole congregation and fails to organize and direct the whole membership.

An Important But Difficult Work of the Minister

While we are discussing the minister's work, we would add this word: It is perhaps the minister's place, together with other workers, to so guide and safeguard the work of all that the result may be converts won to *Christ,* rather than to the minister, to the evangelist or to the congregation. The appeal to "unite with *our* church" because of its standing, advantages or whatever, should be discouraged at all points. The appeal that evangelist, minister and personal workers must be urged to make is acceptance of Christ as Saviour, because He is the only Saviour from sin. In taking the confession, the minister too often elaborates on the nobility of the one making the confession, as though such a step were doing God a favor and paying Christ a compliment, rather than a confession of guilt and an acceptance of a Saviour. It might be well even to emphasize the fact that there is no such term in the New Testament as "joining the church." The whole emphasis is on accepting Christ as Saviour, obeying Him as Lord and serving Him in His church. Obedience that leads to forgiveness and salvation places us in the list of the saved, and God adds us to Christ's church.

It Doesn't Matter

How Deep Your Well Is

If There Is No Water In It

CHAPTER V

PREPARATORY WORK OF THE ELDERS AND BIBLE-SCHOOL SUPERINTENDENT

"Feed the flock of God which is among you" (1 Pet. 5: 2).

The Eldership

In the ages in which Roman Catholicism was developing, the church drifted entirely from the New Testament plan of lay leadership by elders and developed the priesthood system. With all the restoring of New Testament patterns by Luther, Calvin, Campbell and all others since, we have never yet succeeded in fully restoring a real New Testament eldership. There may be exceptions, but the fact that there are exceptions proves the rule. In many places the idea of "authority over the flock" has developed without many, if any, of the New Testament qualifications or works on which such authority, as indicated in the New Testament, rested. In fact, the New Testament does not so much indicate *authority* of the elders as it does indicate *responsibility*. The shepherd is responsible for the sheep, to feed and guard as well as herd. The authority indicated in the New Testament is not one of official status, but only the authority which goes with character, experience and ability to lead, shepherd and guide. An elder with these qualifications will always find himself in the lead without the necessity for asserting official authority. No higher honor can be conferred on earth than to be made an elder in the church of God.

[106]

Responsibility of Elders

The very nature of the eldership indicates the work and responsibilities of an elder. Elders are the bishops, that is to say, the shepherds of the flock. They are responsible, not only for the watchcare, but for the increase of the flock. Elders have no right to let a flock die out. They are as responsible for the lambs as for the sheep. The very nature of an elder's obligations points to a leading interest in the Bible school. In fact, the responsibility does not end here. The good shepherd goes far to find the sheep that is lost. There is no greater responsibility that can rest upon a man in this world than that of being an elder in a church of the Lord Christ. If we stop to vision our report to Christ when we stand before Him face to face, it will help us to understand and appreciate our responsibility as elders. An elder indifferent either to the straying sheep or to the lost sheep and lambs is not a New Testament elder. All that has been said indicates most pointedly that there is something very definite for the elders to do when a soul-saving campaign is being planned. An active interest on the part of elders in every phase of the work is in order. This begins with the choosing of the evangelist and runs through all the phases of work mentioned, and by no means ends when the evangelistic campaign ends.

The Bible-school Superintendent

In a way, the work of the Bible-school superintendent and the work of all teachers is a delegated work. The minister, i. e., the evangelist and the elders are responsible for the spiritual teaching and instruction from the Word of God. Where done by others, it is a more or less delegated function, but the elders are yet responsible for what is taught in the name of the church and for the way of teaching which will increase the flock as well as feed it for healthy development. Therefore, the relationship of the Bible-school superintendent and the elders should be most intimately co-operative and harmonious. There is no place in the whole work of the church where this co-operation ought to stand out more pronouncedly than in the harvest time of the church, the evangelistic campaign.

Specific Things To Do in Preparation

We mention a few of the many things that the superintendent and elders may well plan and carry out aside from their participation as individuals in many of the things mentioned in former chapters:

(1) *Aligning the Bible-school teachers in the campaign.* Let them call the teachers together, first, to commit them thoroughly to the campaign, and second, to plan a course in intensive doctrinal training for the teachers so that they may be better equipped to pass this teaching on to their classes. (See materials, pages 135-164.)

(2) *Providing doctrinal courses to be used in classes.* Help the teachers to plan or choose definite doctrinal courses, suitable to their age groups, to be used as supplementary teaching in the classes prior to the revival.

(3) *Preparing the teachers to be soul-winners.* Promote interest in and ability for soul-winning among all teachers. Show them that they are not only instructors, but evangelists for Christ.

A faithful lady teacher of young people, from Kansas, suggests the following which she has used successfully: "Before the class, have a placard printed, 'Christ for All.' Then start toward a goal of winning the members to Christ until the card may be turned over and read, 'All for

Christ.' The Christian members of the class take an active interest in leading others to obey the Saviour."

(4) *Learning to know the pupils.* Lead each teacher to study every pupil and become thoroughly familiar with every individual, from the standpoint of church relationship and religious needs.

(5) *Inspiring teachers to reach the unreached.* Show the teachers that the Bible school is the longest-reaching arm of the church, and commit every teacher to an immediate and systematic effort to find and bring the unreached into her class.

(6) *Securing prospect lists through the teachers.* Ask every teacher to furnish names and data on the church relationship of the people in the homes represented in her entire class.

(7) *Arousing general expectancy.* Plan to keep the revival meeting before the whole Bible-school group and to arouse expectancy and interest.

(8) *Enrolling workers for definite tasks.* Use the classes for enrolling ready groups of workers; boys and girls for distributing advertising; women for calling and distributing invitations; adults and young people for assistance in the census, in the choir and for clerical work, such as letter writing, mimeographing and addressing; automobile drivers with their cars for bringing shut-ins or others to the meetings, etc.

(9) *Eliminating conflicting enterprises.* Use the influence of the Bible school to help in relegating all social and other enterprises to the extreme rear, and in putting the revival first of all things while the meeting is going on.

These are but some of the important things the elders and Bible-school superintendents can plan and carry out together in preparation for the campaign.

CHAPTER VI

MEN AND THE CAMPAIGN

"Remember this, and show yourselves men" (Isa. 46: 8).

Where Distinctions Are To Be Made

In much of the Christian life and work for Christ, no distinction of sex should be made. Both male and female have souls, both must hear and obey the same gospel, both must grow in grace and knowledge of the truth, both must render service, not only for their reward by and by, but also for their spiritual health and vigor here.

However, in some of the work of the church, in order to do all things "decently and in order" and to the best advantage for the cause of Christ, there are some distinctions of sex that can well be made. All recognize this principle as applied to the eldership. Largely it is made in regard to the preaching ministry and the nursing ministry. One falls largely to men; the other, almost exclusively to women. Thus we see that there is a recognized distinction, and this distinction can advantageously be made in the work of a local congregation.

Some Facts of History and Life

A few facts will help to make plain why certain work is best performed by men. Here are some of the facts:

(1) *Old Testament example*. Under the Jewish regime men were wholly in charge and in the lead in religious matters, both in the synagogue and in the home.

(2) *New Testament example.* In Jesus' day and in the early church, the count was made as of men. See Matt. 14:21 and Acts 4:4. Women and children were taken for granted or mentioned incidentally. This would indicate that men assumed the responsibility for the work almost exclusively.

(3) *Modern departures.* In modern times, too often the church and its work is looked upon as something "for children and women only." The man of the house counts himself as but a "brother-in-law" to the church, because his wife belongs. Men are willing to attend board meetings and vote, but leave the actual work to the women or to a hired preacher.

(4) *Work which only men can do.* Certain work can be done only by men. If a men's Bible class is to be built up, men only can do it. If the indifferent men of the community are to be reached, they will have to be reached *by men of the church,* if reached at all. Men have an approach to men that no one else has. Laymen have an approach to men that even the minister is denied by the fact of his being a minister.

(5) *Reaching the man reaches the family.* Though women and children frequently can be reached for the church without the man, it is a fact that *if* the man is reached the whole family will almost surely be reached.

A Work for Men

The unquestioned facts above reveal that there is a work for the men of the church that can be done by no one else. We, therefore, enumerate some of the things that the men can best do and should do in preparation for the revival. Two things are to be remembered: One is, that the men can grow in interest in the church only by doing

[111]

definite work in the church, and second, that the reason more men do not do actual work in the church is that they have not been individually assigned to specific pieces of work which they can do. Following are some specific tasks:

(1) *Refurbishing the building.* Call together all the professional and amateur craftsmen, such as carpenters, masons, plasterers, paper hangers, painters, plumbers, electricians or other craftsmen, and form them into a committee to secure any other volunteer help they may need to take charge of and do the job of thoroughly refurbishing the churchhouse and furnishings in readiness for the meeting. Here is men's work and men will do it if asked. If they run out of material, their interest will lead them to take up a collection and provide the paint, nails or whatever is needed.

(2) *Building the men's class.* Give the men's Bible class a definite quota of increase as their share in building up the Bible-school attendance in preparation for the meeting.

(3) *Men and the census.* Throw the men into the census-taking, along with the women and young people.

(4) *Listing and contacting prospects.* Ask the men to furnish you the names and addresses of all men in the community who are not actively tied up with the church or are not attending a Bible school. See that this list is furnished, then induce the men to make no less than six calls on each unreached man, changing callers, but keeping at it with persistence until the man has been brought out. Men will call if asked to make a specific call. Pair the timid and inexperienced with the more experienced. Instruct these men to tell those on whom they call about the coming meeting.

[112]

(5) *Devising a men's program for the men's class.* Choose a group of men to help work out an all-around program for the men's class, which will draw men and hold men at least until they are landed in the gospel net. This program includes general exercises in the class and week-time enterprises.

(6) *Finding real personal workers.* There are some of the men who can be trained and taught and made into real personal workers. Find out which ones have this ability, pick them out, draw them out, lead them out, train them and then send them out. Send them on specific assignments.

(7) *Men and the choir.* Get more men into the choir. They are an inspiration to other men.

(8) *Trained ushers.* Make up your entire ushering force of men and give them careful training for the work. See page 55ff of this book.

(9) *Use special abilities.* If you discover any men with sign-painting ability, put them to work painting large posters and posting them at every advantageous crossroad. Have the carpenters make the poster boards. See chapter on "Advertising."

(10) *An automobile brigade.* Organize the automobile squad to assist in advertising the meeting and bringing people to the meeting who can not or might not come otherwise.

(11) *A suggestion committee.* Appoint a committee, called the "suggestion committee," whose job is to think of and suggest other things the men can do that are not suggested here.

CHAPTER VII

THE WOMEN'S WORK FOR THE CAMPAIGN

"And this is the promise that he hath promised us, even eternal life" (1 John 2: 25).

Work That Is Strictly Suitable for Women

The work that women can do in preparation for an evangelistic campaign is decidedly important. It is true that much of it consists of participation with others in the census, the preliminary invitational calling, certain phases of putting the building in clean and inviting shape and other like phases. There are some things, however, that fall to the women only. Among these would be the making of a supply of baptismal robes and cloths, assisting lady candidates for baptism, and teaching interested prospects. In this chapter we shall discuss some of the things that the women can do better than anyone else, and mention again the phases in which they merely participate with others.

Invitational Calling

In former chapters, especially in the one on "Advertising," it was urged that sufficient pieces of attractive advertising be provided so that one piece might be in *every* home in the whole territory, and that no piece of the material be wasted. This is important. However, the *manner* in which this material is delivered is even more important. The intention is to get results. Merely to *toss* these revival bills at people lacks many things to make the advertising lay hold on people's minds and hearts. If the bills are thrown on porches, placed in mail boxes or distributed in some other way by boys and girls, more than half the effect has been lost.

We urge that as nearly as possible all the women of the church be asked to help make this first round. Carefully district the territory by blocks, send the women, two by two, on clearly defined assignments of territory, such that they can cover their assignments in not more than two hours. Instruct them to call at *every* door, knock, and when the lady of the house opens up, they are to introduce themselves as Mrs. B———— and Mrs. G———— of First Church, and say, "We have stopped to tell you of the beginning of a good revival meeting at First Church next Sunday." Add a short bit of detail about the evangelist, tell the lady you would be pleased to have her attend, together with all the members of her family. Listen for any reply that might indicate interest and a prospect. Do not write the data down there, but do write down name, address and facts as soon as you are out of sight. However, after extending a gracious, personal invitation, say, "I am leaving you one of the announcements." Hand her the poster and leave. Do not go in for a call.

If this piece of work is done by the women of the church, it will multiply the pulling power of the printed matter by three or four. Here is one of the first, very important things women can do better than any one else in preparation for the revival.

Preparation of Baptismal Robes

It is highly important that every church be prepared to baptize people promptly and properly. Baptism is a burial in semblance of Christ's burial and should be done with all the decorum and reverence possible. Nothing ought ever to be allowed to mar or detract from the sacredness, seriousness and solemnity of a burial in baptism. More than that, a baptism should be performed promptly. It is too important to put off for personal convenience, need of proper apparel or for any other reason. Let the men have the baptistery or place for baptism ready and in order. The women can secure the material and make a sufficient number of robes so that the church may be ready for a baptismal service at any time. Further on we give detailed suggestions as to how a proper robe may be made.

Why Robes Are Advisable

If baptismal robes are properly made from the right material, they may be used without any other apparel. Thus one can come forward at any service, and without waiting to provide additional clothing can be baptized, using the robe. Also, it is true, especially in the case of women, that ordinary dress is wholly unsuited for baptism. It is also true that, if the church does not prepare to guide in the matter of proper apparel for the baptismal service, but leaves it to the judgment of wholly inexperienced people, candidates will all too often be sent to the baptistery with quite unsuitable clothing for the service. Any impropriety or mistake embarrasses the candidate, distracts her attention from the thoughts of her obedience to the Saviour and obscures the beautiful lesson which a properly performed baptism can teach to the onlooker.

Candidates properly robed have much more assurance and calm, and their baptism is much easier for the minister to perform in a dignified and reverent manner. Away with the thought that robes are for display or that they suggest formality. They are to prevent display and to help focus the attention of all on the face of the candidate, and the thought of all on the spiritual significance of the service. We believe robes to be as advisable for the small church as for the large, and for the open baptism as for one performed in a baptistery.

The Actual Making of the Robes

Aside from the practical use of the baptismal robes themselves, the very enterprise of making them helps to create expectancy and arouse interest.

Do *not* use waterproof material or a material that tends to become either waterproof or airproof when wet. All cotton goods has this tendency. Anything water- or airproof holds the air and brings the material to the top in a large floating bubble of cloth when the candidate is lowered. Use porous wool goods. The cloth being wool, the water does not cling and stop up the pores. The air escapes easily whether the cloth be wet or dry. A medium grade black or dark blue wool crepe is illustrative of a wholly suitable material. Whatever material is used, be sure that the color is strictly fast. A robe of suitable material, properly designed and weighted, never floats or bubbles. It falls and drapes itself automatically, and conceals the form perfectly. Being porous, it admits the air and prevents clinging when the candidate is raised.

The drawings, marked measurements and specifications found on pages 187, 188, of the appendix, will, we hope, enable any group of ladies to make these robes. No pattern is needed except for the yoke. All other cuts are absolutely straight. Following the yoke details and measurements, a yoke pattern should be cut.

Assisting at the Baptistery

Baptism is a sacred ordinance, but the candidate is naturally wholly inexperienced. In the case of all girls and women who come forward, let a trained and specially appointed deaconess or other good woman of the church greet them at once, extend a welcome and offer her services and counsel. First, let her discuss, with the one who has come forward, the details of time and necessary arrangements and equipment for her baptism. When the time comes, this same trained woman should be present in, and in charge of, the dressing room. Nervousness on the part of the candidates frequently develops into levity, and levity into flippancy, which is out of keeping with the occasion. Let the deaconess maintain an air of reverence and seriousness by her guidance of the conversation. She may well have a word of prayer with candidates just before their baptism. It is important that she supervise, or at least carefully inspect, the apparel of each to see that no chance is left for any untoward happening due to an oversight in preparation. If need be, she may assist the candidate to, and up out of the baptistery, all the while adding the quiet word that assures, quiets and guides the thoughts of the candidate. Her duties end only when the last candidate is reclothed and the dressing room and robes cared for. Here again is an important work for the good women of the church.

Work in the Choir

To fill a place in the choir is real work if done regularly, consistently and with the spirit of service. If a thoroughly dependable group can be enrolled for the music of the campaign, a most important problem of the meeting has been solved. Nothing hampers the success of a meeting more than late or irregular players and singers. Here again is a place where both the younger and older women can render a real and important service. Enroll. Enroll for the duration of the meeting. Be as dependable about being in your place on time as is the evangelist. Consecrate yourself to the service. Maintain a serious interest. Sing with a prayer that the singing may prepare people to obey the gospel.

The Work of Hostess

In the chapter on "The Cottage Prayer Meeting," we mentioned the work which the women may do as hostesses for the cottage prayer meetings. There is one phase of the hostess service against which a warning should be sounded. In a large number of cases it is necessary that the evangelist be entertained in a home or homes. Where this entertainment is to be provided, it is usually and quite properly put in the hands of a committee of the women. Their one fault is that they do their work far too well. A constant succession of two special meals each day is provided by assigning the evangelist to one home for the noon hour and to another for the evening meal each day. Each lady provides a big meal, and to be courteous the evangelist must show his appreciation by partaking heartily. No man on earth can stand this day after day and week after week and do good work.

The evangelist is there to do a hard piece of work. Do not ruin the meeting by entertaining and feeding him to death. Give him a quiet room, where he may be alone at times for rest, study, and planning. Give him a chance to eat what is good for him or to refrain from eating when he deems it best.

Tasks in Which the Women Participate with Others

There is not one task that we have mentioned in the book but what women may have a helpful part in, except the work of the men in reaching men. We need not repeat the discussions here of what is to be done and how, for that has been covered in former chapters. In this chapter we have attempted to touch only those tasks particularly suited to women only.

Control of Interferences with the Meeting

We list the control of enterprises, which may interfere with the meeting, under the work of the women, because they can better control this matter than anyone else. However, whether it be women, men or young people, the rule should be that the meeting comes first. All social and other activities, meetings and clubs, including class meetings and meetings of any and all other church organizations, should be postponed unless such meetings can be made use of to promote the revival meeting. If the evangelistic meeting succeeds, all these groups will reap results that will be worth more to them than could accrue from the regular activities. Besides all this, it should be kept in mind that all church organizations are but means to make possible the very thing for which the evangelistic meetings stand.

God Could Conceivably Pardon

an Unwashed Dish

If You Could Show Him

a Saved Soul Instead

CHAPTER VIII

USING THE YOUTH OF THE CHURCH

"Let no man despise thy youth" (1 Tim. 4: 12).

Why Use the Young People?

There are a number of reasons why the plans for the revival should comprehend using the young people and the boys and girls. Among these reasons is that you will need the interest of the boys and girls and young people if you hope to reach other youth. The interest of your boys and girls is built up and held by giving them something definite and worth while to do. Another reason is that interested boys and girls constitute a most valuable advertising media, if so used. You make friends of the youth by giving them something to do rather than by what you do for them. If the young people and boys and girls of a whole community are your friends, you may depend upon it that you are going to be favorably known and favorably publicized in the community. Lastly, if you would have the youth to grow in grace and knowledge of the truth, give them a part in the work.

A Part in the Advertising Campaign

We have urged that the first distribution of printed matter be made, home to home, by the women, extending a personal invitation at the same time. We have suggested that this be done four or five days before the meeting begins. Then follow this up the day before the meeting begins by having a doorknob hanger hung on every door.

Here is a work that can well be done by the boys and girls. Assign each one or each two to a definitely described territory. Print the cards on light cardboard, punch the cards and tie string loops six inches long in each. The card may read, "I am hanging around to remind you ——————" etc. Do not ever pay for this service of distribution, or treat for it. Let it be a service for the church.

Youth Choirs and Drills*

The people are more interested in their children than in any and all else. If possible, devise a means to enroll a very large junior chorus to be used on specified nights. Father and Mother will come to hear Junior sing. Form groups to meet you in the afternoon for intensive Bible teaching and Scripture drills. Exhibit the results on announced evenings. Again the adults will be interested. Last of all in this connection, we urge that an earnest endeavor be made to teach and really win these boys and girls. The opening to many a home and to many a community lies in and through the boys and girls.

Afternoon Services for Youth

A plan that has been widely used, comprehends visiting the public schools and securing the co-operation of the superintendents and teachers in plans for character-building programs. Talk it over with the teachers. If deemed advisable, hand out tickets to each child, for a definite afternoon program. Be ready to lead good singing, do interesting Bible drilling and to talk briefly, though frankly, to the children about right and wrong, God, Christ and the Bible. Sincerely strive to make it exactly what you promised—a character-building program. Take no

* On pages 184ff in the appendix we have given one doctrinal drill which will prove popular and profitable for such a meeting.

advantage. Ordinarily we deem it not best to try to make these afternoon programs evangelistic. Reserve that for the regular services.

Young People's Special Night

Early in the meeting plan for and advertise a special night for young people. Have all your young people help to plan it. If possible, have young people exclusively for the choir. Have others to usher and others to assist from the platform in opening services. Have your young people to list all the young people of the community, and write invitations to attend the Young People's Special Night. A young people's sunrise service or breakfast at the church has been used successfully.

Linking Daily Vacation Bible School with the Evangelistic Campaign

One of our younger ministers from Texas submitted the following suggestion. Plan the daily vacation Bible school to overlap the revival meeting by one week. During the first part of the daily vacation Bible school, one teacher devotes much of her time to the preparation of numbers to be used in the evangelistic meeting. During the last week, the pupils rehearse their work in the daily school, then at night some one of the departments contributes a special demonstration number for the evening service. He adds: "This secured peak attendance from the first, as parents are always interested in such presentations. It constituted incentive to the children in the school, it served as excellent preliminary advertising for the coming meeting, it made the children feel they had a definite part in it. The only warning is to avoid the tendency to 'high pressure' the daily vacation Bible school pupils into mass confession before they are ready."

[123]

CHAPTER IX

PERSONAL WORK IN THE CAMPAIGN

"Study to show thyself approved unto God, a workman that needeth not to be ashamed, rightly dividing the word of truth" (2 Tim. 2: 15).

What Is Personal Work?

Naturally any work done by any person for Christ is personal work. The man who gives his service to fix the furnace so that it will produce heat instead of smoke, and who does it as a matter of service for Christ and the church, has done personal work which has an effective part in helping to win souls. Usually, however, the term "personal work" is applied to that type of work in which a Christian works definitely with and for some other one person, by teaching and persuasion, in an endeavor to win that person to decision for Christ. This kind of work may be done by going quietly to some one during the invitation, or it may be done by going to some person in his home, his office or his shop. Frequently, the term "personal work" is limited to the type of work done by individuals in the audience of a revival during the invitation. In this chapter we shall deal with *personal work* as any definite personal teaching and persuasion, either in the meeting or in the home or shop.

Personal Work in the Home

There are some advantages not to be overlooked in the home call. The prospect has a chance to talk back and thus reveal his difficulties, problems, perplexities or prejudices. Thus the caller may have some idea of what and where the difficulty is that needs to be removed. Also, it is possible to establish a friendly and informal relationship that tends to sympathetic hearing. Lastly, there is more time to do real teaching and Bible reading. Such personal work might be studied under the heads: the approach to people, how to use the Bible, how to lead to decision and how to close the call.

(1) *Approaching people.* Perhaps the most effective and most needed type of personal work is that done by calling directly in the home, shop, store or office. By knowing everything possible about the one to be called on, i. e., his interests, his attitudes, his church relationships or leanings, his family's church relationship, etc., the caller can plan a proper approach. It is well to plan the approach in one's mind. By all means, the approach must be such as not to offend; must be one to gain attention, if possible, and one which wins the interest of the prospect from the very start.*

(2) *Using the Bible.* In these personal calls, always carry your own Bible or Testament, preferably one with which you are so familiar, or which is so thoroughly labeled and marked, that you can readily locate a plain Scripture on any one of the many points or excuses which the prospect may bring up. It is better to read the Bible to a prospect than to quote it from memory. It impresses him more. It is better yet to read the Bible *with* a prospect than to read it *to* him. Ask him to bring out his own Bible and read with you.

(3) *Leading to definite ends.* The first approach in a call may start with almost any interest, such as the pros-

---

* This subject is treated at some length in the book "Personal Evangelism."

pect's business, his fads, his home, his children, his public
interests or whatever. The caller must learn how to listen
as well as talk, but the caller must keep in mind the exact
purpose of the call, and watch for the point on which he
may lay hold and lead as directly as possible to conversation about the church, the Bible, obedience to the gospel,
the reading of the Bible together, or whatever end may
appear to be advisable and to be sought.

(4) *Closing the call.* The nature of the call will determine its close. In some cases a definite pledge may be
secured to make the confession and be baptized at the very
next service. In some cases, especially of shut-ins, the
confession may be taken. In other cases the call may result
in a Bible reading together, which the caller naturally
guides, and may result in an appointment for further Bible
reading together. In some cases the call may lead only
to the opportunity to press an urgent invitation to attend
the services at the church. It is well to determine, if possible, the result which you believe to be achievable, lead to
that point and close the call graciously. By all means,
try to leave before spoiling such good effect as has been
achieved.*

Personal Work by Bible-class Teachers

Every Bible-class teacher, including those of the
Beginners Department and up, should conceive of herself
as a winner of souls, i. e., an evangelist. Even with the
tiniest tots, suggestions may be dropped which will begin
to plant and fix the notion that some day they will obey
the gospel, be baptized, wear the name Christian and work
in the church.

Beginning with the Junior age, the aim should begin

* Forms for cards to be used in this work can be found on page 182.

to be definite and much more immediate. A well-taught Junior is much better prepared to obey the gospel intelligently than hosts of untaught adults. Clear doctrinal teaching is in order, therefore, among all groups above the Primary, with the direct aim of leading to personal decision. The decision must be *personal* and not a group decision. Therefore, it is advisable for the teacher to seek and plan for individual, personal and private conversation with each unreached pupil. It is more effective, both for immediate and for permanent results, than much of the class teaching and exhortation.

Personal Work During the Invitation

Personal work during the invitation is approved by some and disapproved by some. Most of our most skilled evangelists recommend and urge such work. Personally, we believe it to be both legitimate and advisable, provided it is planned and guided. It depends on who does this work and how it is done. Merely to overpersuade an untaught or unrepentant person is not advisable, but there are many cases of people who are taught sufficiently and convinced, who lack and need only a bit of urgent, friendly persuasion and encouragement.

Personal work in an audience during the invitation naturally does not lend itself to much teaching and must, therefore, be of the nature of exhortation and urgency. Only the earnestness, tact and good sense of the worker can determine when to go to some one and add this bit of needed stimulus and assistance to decision. Whatever is done should be done quietly and without ostentation. Stand by the side of the one to whom you talk. Try to be so frank and friendly as to remove any embarrassment. Have as much knowledge of his spiritual and mental status as possible. Have some idea of how you intend to approach him and what you propose to say. If you fail in immediate results, leave with a smile and a happy contact rather than a frown. Never argue. Leave the prospect so you could approach him on the subject if you should meet him anywhere the next day. (Note: On page 182 of the appendix appears the replica of two commitment cards, which we have found valuable for use in personal work in homes and frequently in the audience. Also in the book, "Personal Evangelism," will be found a somewhat more extended treatment of "personal work.")

Personal Work in One's Own Home

Why Christians should have a greater hesitancy about teaching their own and urging them to accept Christ than they have about talking to another is something none of us can explain. This seems to be the fact, however. Is it not also a fact that mothers and fathers will have a greater responsibility for which to answer in regard to the souls of their own children, than for any and all others? Has the Christian wife not a greater responsibility for the soul's safety of her own husband, or the husband for the wife, than for any other one person? When we really believe the truth of the gospel, that the unsaved are lost, can we longer refrain from overcoming our hesitancy to speak to and work for our very own?

That Little Sin of Yours May Be a Little Sin,
But if It Is Large Enough to Cause You
to Reject Christ, It Is Quite as Fatal
as the Greatest Sin on Earth.

CHAPTER X

THE USE OF TRACTS IN EVANGELISM

"But if our gospel be hid, it is hid to them that are lost" (2 Cor. 4: 3).

What Is a Tract?

The dictionary defines a tract as, "A treatise or written discourse, generally short, especially on practical religion." A tract is generally short so that the busy man may read it through quickly. Because of the necessary brevity, the writer has to put his very best in the most concise and pointed way. Writing a tract calls for the very best skill and brains of a writer. Tracts provided by good and wise Christian leaders, therefore, represent their most skilled, condensed and expert work in dealing with some important Bible teaching.

In dealing with objections and problems of prospects, we often have questions raised which we are personally unequipped to answer satisfactorily. We wish we might have at our elbow our minister or some skilled teacher. This is exactly what we can have if we have familiarized ourselves with, and provided ourselves with, a choice selection of the briefest of tracts on the questions most often to be met in personal work. We may immediately call to our assistance the wisest and most expert of our brethren, such as J. W. McGarvey, Isaac Errett and others.

Permanent Work of Tracts

Our oral teaching may soon be forgotten by the hearer. However, if after doing our oral teaching on any phase of Bible truth, we have a tract plainly presenting the Bible teaching on that subject, which we can leave in the hands of the one taught, we leave something to which he can refer and refresh his memory. It will aid him to check on the Bible references, and will stay with him until its work has been done. Things read many times sink in deeper and make a more lasting impression than things heard. The best of tracts may be purchased at very little cost.

Practical for Everybody

Not all are expert in teaching and leading, but any one can use tracts. Many times the conversation is necessarily so brief or so interrupted that it may not be brought to any satisfactory conclusion. A good tract is an ever present help under such circumstances. Tracts may be mailed with a brief personal word. They may be personally handed out or they may be left where the passer-by may pick them up in his spare moments. All the un-Scriptural cults make a very generous and effective use of tracts. Business floods the mail with tracts called "circulars." The business man does not wait for you to come to him, but he constantly comes to you through the mail. Why not use the same wisdom and enterprise for the gospel of Christ?

For Opening and Closing a Conversation

Many willing workers do not know how to open a conversation leading to a discussion of things Christian. Frequently, a tract may be used as the opening which will lead directly to the points in which you wish your hearer to be interested. Likewise, many workers are at a loss to know how to close a really profitable discussion. A well-chosen tract is an ideal means to that end.

To Inform Workers

Again and again, in the chapters of this book, we have come face to face with the need for the *workers* to know the Bible and its teaching on the problems most vital to all men. There is no better plan for becoming familiar with the basic doctrines and the Bible teaching, than by providing ourselves with a plain and carefully written tract on each of these vital teachings. The cost is negligible, and the profit is beyond measure. Such tracts can be secured for from one to three cents each. They contain the best and plainest teachings of our most consecrated and best-informed leaders.

Tracts on Display

A tract is much more liable to do an effective work if the way has been paved for it and an interest aroused in the subject which it treats, before it is handed out. However, there are innumerable instances in which a chance tract has won a soul to Christ.

If tracts are chosen which cover the theme of a particular sermon, and are put on display for free distribution at the close of the service in which that sermon has been preached, they have the advantage of having had the way paved for them. If those remaining are then gathered up and others put on display, fitting the next sermon, much good can be done. The sermon arouses the interest, the tract carries the work home. It is better if one suitable person can be found and chosen to have full charge of all tracts.

PART III
Ammunition for the Campaign

EXPLANATION OF USES OF SECTIONS IN PART THREE

Value of Basic Doctrinal Teaching

A book intended to cover all the phases of preparation for, and carrying out of, an evangelistic campaign would be incomplete without at least some definite material along the line of plain Bible teaching on basic doctrinal themes. The purpose of the material submitted in Part III is to cover a number of needs. Among these are: To indoctrinate the unreached in the Bible school and to prepare them for intelligent decision; to prepare teachers, church officers and all workers, so that they may be equipped and inclined to do clear and suitable doctrinal teaching and personal work, and to refresh the spirits of all with the basic principles of New Testament teaching.

Uses of Section A

Section A, beginning on page 135, is intended to be used as a series of substitute or supplementary lessons in classes or departments containing pupils whom you hope to reach during the meeting. These same lessons may also be used for a week-night class to prepare teachers for doctrinal teaching or to prepare a group of personal workers.

If time is too short to complete the entire series, the later chapters could be deferred until after the meeting.

Uses of Section B

After reshaping to fit your local situation, Section B, Part III, page 165, is intended to be reprinted on tough cardboard, or on thinner sheets which can be pasted in songbooks and used as a regular three-minute, catechetical drill in the general opening service of the Bible school every Sunday for some weeks. Where departments meet separately, the same material can be used by merely changing the copy, which designates the ones who are to ask the questions and the group that is to respond. Part of the value consists in the alertness aroused by the continuous skipping from one officer or group to another. All hear every question and every answer so that all get the benefit of the entire drill. The constant repetition fixes these Scripture truths forever. Copy can be expanded or contracted to suit any local situation.

Uses of Section C

Section C consists of a series comprised of two sayings, and a group of nineteen Scriptures, systematically and climactically arranged. These are copies from a series of charts used most successfully in many meetings for years. They are intended to be painted separately on sign-painter's muslin, handwork with brush, and hung entirely around the auditorium in the order given. Each banner should be separate, and the larger ones about 10-ft. by 3-ft. They may be used before the meeting to indoctrinate members, but they are especially designed to use as a drill to be repeated over and over in the opening exercises during the meeting for the purpose of teaching and fixing in the minds of the unreached these plain, doctrinal teachings.

Use printers ink cut with turpentine or gasoline. On strips 10 feet long and 3 feet wide, the capital letters can be 6 inches high, readable 75 feet away. We have used these charts as a ten-minute drill every night for three weeks and always they have proven successful. They use the eye gate as well as the ear gate. Repetition both fixes and impresses the truth.

These sayings and Scriptures may also be printed in 12 point type at local printery, and inserted or pasted into the songbooks used in the revival. The whole may also be printed of a size to distribute widely as a short tract.

Section A. Ten Brief Doctrinal Studies

CHAPTER I

THE BIBLE AND HOW TO PRESENT IT

"Thy word is truth"—Jesus.

How We Know the Bible Is True

Is the Bible true? Is it the Word of God? If it is not, then we may disregard it, but there is nothing left to guide us. If it is God's Word and true, we all should want to know it, and dare not disregard it.

Following are a few of the many facts showing the Bible to be the Word of God:

1. Its long life and unprecedented circulation indicate that it is different from all other books. It has outlived all other books, and each year, for centuries, has outsold that year's best-seller in all other fields. This it does today. An average of two millions of copies of the Bible have been sold each year during the past century.

2. The fact that it was written by about thirty different men, for the most part unknown to one another, and separated by a period of sixteen hundred years from the first to the last, and yet is a perfectly fitted unit, shows that there was one Mind guiding it all. That could be no other than the mind of God.

3. The many prophecies written down, and then fulfilled to the letter hundreds of years later, indicate that

[135]

their Author was One who could see forward as well as backward. No one but God can do that.

4. Its effect upon man is evidence that it is from God. Nations of people have been changed from savage cannibals to law-abiding, Christian men by the influence of the Bible.

It stands for something that nothing else stands for. To illustrate: Two travelers, in a rough mountain country, were overtaken by night and compelled to seek shelter in a rough mountain cabin. They were shown to an attic that had a loose-board floor. The rough appearance of the place and people made them afraid they would be robbed or murdered. They agreed that one should watch while the other slept. Soon the one watching through the cracks of the floor began to prepare to retire. The other asked why. "There is no danger here," he said; "they are reading the Bible and having prayer down there." There is no other book that would have meant the same.

5. The fact that the Bible always approves what is right and condemns only evil helps to show it is from God.

Why We All Need the Bible

Many of us will never need to know the way to Paris, London or the North Pole, but we all are headed for the future, and need to know the way. Books of geography may tell us the way to many places, but only the Bible tells of the *one* way which *all* must travel. Science may tell us how to live longer and better here, but only the Bible tells us how to live eternally. Money may buy nearly anything here, but all the money in the world can not buy what the Bible offers. Science tries to tell where man came from, but only the Bible tells where man is going, and that is the more important of the two.

Ammunition for the Campaign

How the Bible Presents Its Truth *

The Bible is a group of books, made to fit the spiritual needs of all ages. The thirty-nine books of the Old Testament, made up of the four groups—law, history, poetry and prophecy—were given to fit the needs of the age before Christ came, and to prepare for His coming.

We are living under the New Testament today. It contains twenty-seven books in all, made up of four groups, or kinds, of books as follows:

1. Four Gospels to tell us of Christ, that we may know that He is the Saviour and that there is no other (John 20: 30, 31).

2. The one Book of Acts to tell us what to do to become Christians and be saved (Acts 2: 38).

3. The twenty-one letters to Christians to tell us how to live the Christian life (2 Pet. 1: 5-11).

4. The one Book of Revelation to tell us to keep on living the Christian life, and not give up (Rev. 2: 10).

Every one should know this arrangement of the books of the Bible, and the purpose of each of these groups.

A Fourfold Classification of Scriptures

All Scripture is made up of:

1. Facts to be believed. "No man cometh to the Father, but by me" would illustrate.

2. Commands to be obeyed. "Repent, and be baptized" is one illustration.

3. Promises to those who believe and obey. "There is no condemnation to them which are in Christ" is one promise.

---

* The four-finger drill starting on page 184 of the appendix will be found helpful at this juncture.

4. Warnings to be heeded. "Fear him who is able to destroy both soul and body" is one warning.

A Difficulty Removed

There is a twofold feature of the Scriptures which, if understood, makes understanding of the teaching easier. In the saving of the soul there is God's part and man's part. Hence, in the Bible is a revelation of man's part and of God's part. Man's part is, and must be, simple and plain. God's part is naturally difficult for us to understand. We need not stumble here, however, for if we do our part, God will certainly fulfill His part.

CHAPTER II

THE DIVINE PLAN

"Know the truth and the truth shall make you free"—Jesus.

Can We Know for Sure What to Do To Be Saved? Where Can We Find Out?

The Bible plan of salvation is plain. Confusion begins when men add to the Bible teaching.

1. The Bible is the only source of information on what to do to be saved. If the Bible does not reveal a plain, sure way, then there is no known way. The Bible does reveal a plain way. (Read Mark 16:16.)

2. Man's part is, and must be, plain. Though God's part may be deep and many times mysterious, we need not stumble if what *we* are to do is plain. To hear and believe the Word; to repent; to confess our faith in Christ with our mouths before men; to be buried in baptism; to

wear the name "Christian"; to assemble with other Christians; to break bread; to pray; these are clearly stated things for us to do.

The Bible Plan Is a Generous Plan

Many people, young people especially, think that to become a Christian means only to give up something—to make sacrifices. The fact is that it is almost entirely a matter of receiving benefits which we could not get from any other source.

Illustration—If a tramp should be asked to give up the dirt on his face, that would be giving up something, but if he is to receive a large, fine farm in exchange, it would be no sacrifice. If God asks us to give a bit of time here in this life, but offers eternal life as a reward, would it be counted as giving or receiving?

What God Does and Offers

We can here but summarize a few of the things which God does for us and which we could not do for ourselves.

1. God does what neither man nor money nor science can do.

2. God gave His only Son to die for our sins, and go into the grave and conquer death for us (John 3:16).

3. God tells us plainly what we are to do to be saved.

4. God offers forgiveness if we be willing and obedient (Mark 16:16).

5. God adds us to the church, and promises to raise us from the dead and add us to the list of the saved (Acts 2:41 and Rev. 21:27).

6. God bestows the name "Christian," and promises it shall be a mark of safety (Rev. 22:4).

7. God gives us eternal life and heaven, which no one else can bestow (Rom. 6:23).

What Man Is Asked To Do. A Plain Way

The New Testament makes it decidedly plain that there is something that man must do (read Matt. 7:21).

1. The first step: Man must hear God's Word. Refusal or neglect to hear will not be a sufficient excuse (read Rom. 10:17).

2. The second step: Faith in Christ with the whole heart, i. e., sincere belief of God's Word about Christ (read Heb. 11:6).

3. Third step: Repentance of sin against Christ. One might be sorry for, and repent of, the sin of disregarding a neighbor or an earthly father or brother, but God also asks for repentance of the sin of disregarding Christ (read Acts 17:30).

Repentance is *decision* to accept God's way. Any one can repent now if he will. Repentance is a silent, mental act over which we have full control.

4. Fourth step: Open confession of faith in Christ with the mouth before men (read Matt 10:32 and Rom. 10:10).

5. Fifth step: Burial with Christ by baptism (Acts 2:37, 38; Rom. 6:3, 4; Col. 2:12, and Gal. 3:27; Matt. 28:18-20).

6. Sixth step: The Christian life.

There is one book, "Acts," to tell how to become Christians; there are twenty-one books—the letters, or Epistles —to tell how to live the Christian life (read Romans 12 and 2 Pet. 1:5-11).

7. Seventh step: Continuing faithful to the end (Rev. 2:10).

CHAPTER III

WHAT DOES GOD REQUIRE US TO BELIEVE AND WHY?

"Thou art the Christ, the Son of the living God"—Peter.

God Does Require Belief

God not only requires faith, i. e., definite belief, but He makes plain as to what it is that is necessary for us to believe in order to be saved:

1. It has been made plain, in the preceding chapter, that God absolutely requires "faith"; i. e., belief of God's Word, which presents Jesus as the only Saviour (see Heb. 11:6): "Without faith it is impossible to please him." In recounting the seven steps in the process of salvation, we found "faith" to be set at the very beginning.

In this study we want to find exactly what it is that God requires us to believe, and why He requires us to believe it. Some think they can not believe, because they have been trying to believe something God never required any one to believe, and because they do not know clearly what it is that God *does* require.

2. It should be kept in mind that God is not *forcing* any one to believe.. God wants us all to be saved. "He is not willing that any should perish." Therefore, He wants us to believe, and makes it plain that we must *if we would be saved.* However, He will not force any one to be saved, and so does not force any one to believe. To illustrate, nature does not force us to eat, but makes it plain that, if we would live, we must eat.

Can We Believe?

Emphatically, we can believe. Any one can believe what God requires us to believe, but just as emphatically,

[141]

one can not believe all the things that men teach that we must believe. It is there that the whole trouble in believing occurs.

Exactly What Does God Require Us to Believe?

God asks us to believe in Christ. To make it quite possible to do this, He gave a perfect One, a Christ in whom not even His most persistent enemies have claimed to find a fault. Is it difficult to believe in one in whom there is no discoverable fault? If you knew a person who was perfect, according to your best ideas of perfection, would you not be compelled to believe in that one? Would it require any effort to believe? Hence God gave us a Saviour who:

1. Gave us flawless teaching.

2. Perfectly lived His perfect teaching.

3. Perfectly fulfilled the age-long prophecies about Him.

4. Gave teaching that has withstood the test of ages (read John 7:17).

5. Gave us abundant evidence upon which to believe in Him (John 20:30, 31).

How Does This Faith or Belief Come?

The heavenly Father deals with us as rational human beings. If He asks us to believe something, He gives us convincing evidence upon which to base our belief.

1. "So then faith cometh by hearing, and hearing by the word of God" (Rom. 10:17). Faith in Christ comes just as faith in anybody comes—by having good evidence and knowing that evidence. He who knows Christ will believe in Him.

2. It is to be remembered that it is not *mere belief* that God requires, but belief *in Christ*. Belief with all the

[142]

heart in self or some one else or some one's idea will not save.

Why Does God Require Belief in Christ?

The question may arise as to why it is that God so insistently makes belief in Christ a first and absolute condition of salvation.

1. God requires belief in Christ for the same reason you would require faith in a bank before you would entrust your money to it. It would be senseless to expect people to trust or obey Christ unless they believe in Him.

2. Because, without faith, baptism would be a farce, repentance impossible and confession a hypocrisy. Therefore, without faith it is impossible to please Him (Heb. 11:6).

CHAPTER IV

THE TURNING POINT

"Except ye repent, ye shall all likewise perish"—Jesus.

What Is Meant by Repentance?

Repentance is usually defined as that sorrow for sin that leads to a definite decision to renounce it for the right. In this study we shall rather present repentance as "the decision itself."

1. The gospel plan is a plan for *all*. *"All have sinned, and come short of the glory of God"* (Rom. 3:23). "Except ye repent, ye shall *all* likewise perish" (Luke 13:3). "The times of this ignorance God hath overlooked; but now commandeth *all men every where* to repent" (Acts 17:30). "Repent, and be baptized *every one* of you in the name of Jesus Christ" (Acts 2:38). This *all* takes in every one—deep-dyed sinners and folks like our Juniors,

[143]

whose lives are not deep in sin. It comprehends all who can hear and understand His Word.

2. To repent, therefore, seems to be something that even the apparently and relatively innocent need to do. What do we mean, then, by that step called "repentance"? Though repentance must follow after a knowledge of the Word and grow out of sorrow for whatever sins may have been committed, yet "repentance itself" is that *decision* to yield to and follow God's way instead of one's own way. This, *all* need to do—all who are old enough to hear and believe—deep-dyed sinners and the relatively innocent.

3. Repentance is an inward *decision* to change, to act on something that up to this time we have not acted on, to say "yes" to something to which we have been saying "no," to go forward rather than backward or stand still. It is, therefore, something *all* can do. It is something all are commanded to do.

Illustration—Repentance is "an about face" from whatever is not right. It is not right to keep on rejecting Christ, therefore, we "about face" and accept Him. It is not right to keep on saying "no" to His calls, therefore, we "about face" and say "yes." It is wrong not to obey Christ, so we turn about and obey Him. We have not treated Him well, whom God sent, and that is sin. We should be sorry for it and decide to accept, obey and serve Him and thus treat Him as we should treat Him. That is repentance toward Christ, or Bible repentance. Sorrow for ordinary misdeeds is valuable only if it *leads to repentance*. It is the repentance, not the sorrow that counts.

4. Many think that repentance is a getting rid of sin in preparation for accepting Christ. Repentance is a decision to accept Christ and follow Him, and thus use His way to get rid of sin.

[144]

Necessity for Repentance

God plainly *commands* repentance. There can be no room for discussion as to its importance, for to question a plain command of God is to question and defy God.

1. Repentance is one of the God-given steps in the gospel plan of salvation. No God-given step is to be left out.

2. It is a definite, plain command of God. "He commandeth," not recommendeth, repentance (Acts 17:30).

Possible for Every One

Some think that they *can not*, of their own accord, repent. Since God commands *all* to repent *now*, it must be something that any one can do, and do promptly. We believe the foregoing has made it plain that it is entirely possible for any one who wants to, to do exactly what God has told all to do, i. e., to repent *now*.

Repentance Toward Christ

One might be sorry for having done wrong to a pet dog. He might decide to quit treating the dog cruelly, make amends for former ill-treatment, and in the future treat him kindly. That would be repentance toward the dog. Yet the same person might go on badly treating his horse or his neighbor or his wife or his father. He might repent toward each of these, in turn, and yet go on treating Christ with unfairness and injustice by disregarding and disobeying Him. When we repent toward Christ, decide to treat Him rightly, we shall then at the same time begin to treat all others as we should. It is repentance toward Christ that God requires. To repent toward Christ means a definite decision to accept Him and begin to follow Him. Following Christ we can not do harm to others.

[145]

Repentance the Turning Point

Repentance takes place in the heart. It is a mental decision unseen by others, but absolutely necessary to one who would be saved.

1. True Bible repentance is the turning point. One may hear the Scripture and believe its truths, but it avails nothing if he stops there. Repentance is the decision to make use of the hearing and believing.

2. Repentance determines what is to follow. If we truly repent, we shall gladly and promptly confess Christ and be baptized. If we do not repent, we either will not confess and obey, or, if we do, it will mean nothing.

The Time to Repent

The heavenly Father not only tells us to repent, but tells us *when* to repent. The when is as much a part of the command as any other part of it. He commands us to repent "now." When God says "now," and we say "not now," it is due to a disobedient heart just as much as to say "no" when God tells us to say "yes." *"Now* is the accepted time—now is the day of salvation" (2 Cor. 6:2. God knows the importance of *now.* Notice the emphatic words—"God," "Commandeth," "All," "Everywhere," "Repent," "Now."

CHAPTER V

THE FIRST OPEN STEP—CONFESSION

"And that every tongue should confess that Jesus Christ is Lord"—Paul.

The First Public Step

Faith, or believing, is naturally an inward matter. One may believe silently. Repentance is, again, an inward affair. One repents or decides silently. However, in the gospel plan, God asks for some things in the open and before all the world. Confession of faith in Christ, with the mouth, before men, is the first such step. Jesus said (Matt. 10:32): "Whosoever therefore shall confess me before men, him will I confess also before my Father which is in heaven." In Rom. 10:10, Paul tells us: "With the mouth confession is made unto salvation." Peter, at Christ's request, openly states his faith (Matt. 16:16).

A Test of Faith, Courage and Purpose

While we may not know all of Christ's purpose in asking us to confess our faith in Him openly, yet it would seem that He has given us two open tests of our faith and our repentance. These are confession and baptism. They are tests of our conviction, of our sincerity, of our courage and of our purpose.

A Preparation for What Is to Follow

Confession is not only the next logical and Scriptural step following repentance, but it is the logical and Scriptural step leading to what is to follow.

1. Confession is a preparation for baptism, for thus we declare our purpose before God and man before we enter the sacred pool of baptism to be buried to the old life, and raised to walk the new.

2. It also prepares us for future needs. If we thus exercise our courage, it will strengthen our courage for the trials, temptations and duties that follow.

A Test of Obedience

Confession is a demonstration of our willingness to obey God's will.

[147]

1. Confession, being the first public, personal act for Christ, becomes, in a way, the first test of our obedience, of our willingness to do His will. We thus show to God, to men and to ourselves that we are willing to obey His commands.

2. It prepares us for future obedience. So long as we are unwilling to submit to this simple test of obedience, we are certainly not prepared for any of the future acts of obedience. On the other hand, if we confess our faith openly, this simple act makes it much easier to take each of the future steps of obedience.

An Act with a Promise

It will be recalled that all Scripture consists of facts to be believed, commands to be obeyed, promises of blessings to be received and warnings to be heeded. Confession is an act which carries a promise. "Whosoever therefore shall confess me before men, him will I confess also before my Father which is in heaven" (Matt. 10:32). When Christ confesses us as His in that great day, it means we *are* His, we are "in Him." "There is . . . no condemnation to them which are in Christ Jesus" (Rom. 8:1).

The Only Confession Needed

The open confession of faith in Christ is the whole and only confession of faith that God, Christ and the Bible require in becoming a Christian. It covers everything, and leaves out nothing that is necessary. Of course, we would not mean to suggest that once is to be the only time we should make this good confession, for we are in many ways to confess Him every day of our lives. If we believe that Jesus is the Christ, why should we not make that confession with our mouths before men?

CHAPTER VI

BIBLE FACTS ABOUT BAPTISM

"As many as have been baptized into Christ have put on Christ"—Paul.

Questions Worth Answering

Is baptism important or unimportant?

Is baptism a mere form or mere outward act?

Is baptism something to be settled by personal preference, personal opinion, personal conscience or by the Word of God? Are the Scriptures plain in their teaching on this subject?

Is Baptism Important?

God, Christ and the Bible leave no doubt as to the importance of baptism. Read the following Scriptures:

1. Jesus, the Son of God, commanded it (Matt. 28: 18-20). Is it important to obey a command of the Saviour?

2. Jesus considered it so important that He walked about seventy miles to be baptized (Mark 1:9-11).

3. God's Holy Spirit, speaking through the Scriptures, teaches it again and again (Acts 2, 8, 9 and many other places).

4. *Every* New Testament instance of conversion either commands or mentions baptism. (See the examples in Acts 2, 8, 9, 10 and 16.)

5. God's chosen messengers, the apostles, taught and definitely commanded it.

Baptism must be very important whether we understand its importance or not; for, to make it unimportant, we should have to disregard all the authority and teaching of God, Christ and the Bible, mentioned above.

What Is Christian Baptism? Are the Scriptures Plain?

The Scripture plainly describes every step in the process of being baptized, and uses language that can be easily understood.

1. The Scriptural description of baptism:
   - (a) "Baptized *in* Jordan" (i. e., in water) (Mark 1:5-9).
   - (b) "Much water" (John 3:23).
   - (c) "Came to the water" (Acts 8:36).
   - (d) "Went down *into* and came *up out* of the water" (Acts 8:36-39).
   - (e) "Buried with him by baptism" (Rom. 6:4; Col. 2:12).
   - (f) "Raised [or resurrected]" (Rom. 6:4, 5).

Could the Word of God make any clearer every move in that sacred act called baptism?

2. The word "baptize" when used by Jesus and the apostles, meant just what the above describes, a burial in water. If Jesus had meant sprinkle or pour, He would have used the word *rantizo,* which meant "sprinkle," or *cheo,* which meant "pour." He used the word *baptidzo,* which meant "dip."

Who Should Be Baptized? Should Infants Be Baptized? Should Unbelievers Be Baptized?

Not only do the Scriptures make plain what is meant by baptism, but they likewise make plain who it is that is to be baptized.

1. The Scriptures make plain, not only the action, but also the design of and proper subjects for baptism. The first definite command is, "Repent and be baptized." Infants can not repent, and unbelievers naturally will

not. Therefore, neither infants nor unbelievers are included.

2. The household baptisms. Some have thought that because the Scriptures tell of whole households that were baptized, infants were baptized. Acts 10—Cornelius: "*All* heard" the Word; "*All* magnified God"; "*All* were baptized." Infants can not hear the Word and praise God, so there were no infants in this household.

Acts 16—Household of Lydia: Later they are all spoken of as "brethren," who were comforted by the Word of God. There could have been no infants among them if old enough to be comforted by the Word of God.

Acts 16—The Philippian Jailer: "All heard," "All believed," "All were baptized," "All rejoiced." Infants could not have done these things.

1 Cor. 1:16—The household of Stephanas. The fifteenth verse of the sixteenth chapter tells that two years later "they had addicted themselves to the ministry." Therefore, no one of them was an infant two years before.

3. Repentant believers are to be baptized. In Acts 18:8, Paul says: "Many of the Corinthians *hearing believed,* and were baptized." Acts 2:41: "They then that received his word were baptized." Verse 38, they had been told to "repent and be baptized." Repentant believers are the only ones to be baptized, according to the Scripture.

What Baptism Means

Baptism is not merely an act of obedience to a command. It has an important and beautiful significance.

1. Baptism is, first of all, an act of obedience to Christ.

2. It is an open declaration of our acceptance of Him.

3. It represents our entry *into* Christ and His church that we may be saved (Gal. 3:27; Rom. 8:1).

[151]

4. It represents the burial to the *OLD,* and resurrection to the *NEW.*

Buried to the *OLD* life:
  - (a) Out of Christ.
  - (b) Out of the church.
  - (c) Unforgiven.
  - (d) Without promise.
  - (e) Life of disobedience.
  - (f) Life in sin.
  - (g) With death and the grave as the end.

Raised to the *NEW* life:
  - (a) In Christ.
  - (b) In the church.
  - (c) Forgiven.
  - (d) With all promises.
  - (e) Life of obedience.
  - (f) Life of service.
  - (g) With eternal life and heaven as the end.

CHAPTER VII

THE NAME, DOES IT MAKE ANY DIFFERENCE?

"Whatsoever ye do in word or deed, do all in the name of the Lord Jesus"—Paul.

Does the Name We Wear and the Name by Which We Call the Church Make Any Difference? Does the Bible Give Any Clear Teaching on the Matter of the Name?

The fact is that the Bible gives very much clear instruction on the subject. If the name makes no difference or little difference, why should the Bible make so much of the name? Ponder the following:

A God-given Name

In the Old Testament prophecy a *"new name"* is promised: "And thou shalt be called by a *new name,* which the mouth of Jehovah shall name" (Isa. 62:2). Since in becoming Christians we become sons and heirs of God as our Father, it is certainly right that He name us. It would certainly be wrong for us to change that name which the Father (God) bestows. We are not left to choose some agreeable or suitable name. God names us and we should wear the name He gives.

The Name He Named

The Bible lays much emphasis upon, and gives much teaching as to, the *name*.

1. The disciples were called "Christians" first in Antioch (Acts 11:26).

2. In Acts 26:28, the name "Christian" next occurs.

3. 1 Pet. 4:16: Peter, the apostle, again uses the name "Christian."

4. In John 17, Jesus again and again prays that we be kept in the name which God had given Him.

5. Again it is referred to in Jas. 2:7 and Rev. 2:13.

Scripture Emphasis of the Name

Christ is all and in all and over all. There is no other name in which there is salvation from sin and death.

1. Salvation in His name (Acts 4:12).

2. Name above every name (Phil. 2:9).

3. Baptized in His name (Acts 2:38).

4. We are to ask for blessings in His name (John 14:13).

5. Blessed when we meet in His name (Matt. 18:20).

6. Unity is in His name (1 Cor. 1:10-13).

7. His name is to be in our foreheads on the judgment day (Rev. 22:4).

When the Word of God makes this much of His name, let us not say, "It makes no difference."

New Testament Names and the Name Above Every Name

While a number of names for Christ's followers appear in the New Testament, it is quite apparent that there is one name which comprehends all others.

[153]

1. There are four chief names used in the New Testament for Christ's followers. They are disciples, brethren, saints, Christians. The word "disciple" means pupil or follower; "brethren" refers to their new relation to each other; "saints" refers to their new, forgiven, cleansed state; "Christian" covers all these relationships in one and links definitely with Christ in addition.

2. Of the four names, the first three are old names long used in the Old Testament. However, when the name "Christian" appears (Acts 11:26) it is a *new* word, a *new* name. It, alone of all, fulfills the prophecy of a *new* name which the mouth of the Lord should name.

The Name of the Church

Christ's name not only is to be worn by His followers, but most certainly is the right and only name for His church.

1. The church is Christ's, and should wear His name (Matt. 16:18). The church is named for its founder, head and owner. It is not left for us to find a name or change the name. God named the church.

2. The church is His body, and should wear His name (Col. 1:24 and Eph. 4:12).

3. The church is His bride, and the bride should wear the groom's name (Rev. 21:2, 9, and 22:17).

CHAPTER VIII

THE CHURCH, WHY BELONG TO IT?

"On this rock I will build my church"—Jesus.

Are the Scriptures Plain as to the Church?

There is, and has been, much confusion about the church. There seem to be many churches and many ways,

so that many earnest people are really confused. They
want to know which is right. Do the Scriptures give us
any plain, sure guidance so we may know most surely
what is right?

Who Owns the Church?

The first thing to know is: Who owns the church?
When we know this, it will clear up much else.

1. The church belongs to Christ. He owns it. It is
His. We do not own it. The church does not belong to
us nor to any group of men. We may belong to the
church, but the church does not belong to us. Then if
we can find what the church which Christ owns is like, we
can go into that and know we are right. Some Scriptures
showing Christ's ownership are:

"My church" (Christ—Matt. 16:18).

"The church of the Lord which he purchased with his
own blood" (Acts 20:28).

2. Since Christ is the only Saviour, He owns the only
church authorized of God. He alone could say what to
do to come into His church. This He has done in the
Scriptures, and has never authorized any one to make new
conditions or change any which He laid down. We can
forget everything else about churches, if we can surely
find and do what He says to do to come into His church.

Where Was His Church Founded?

To recognize a church of Christ, we must know when
and where His church was founded or born. Christ said
He would found *His* church (Matt. 16:18).

History gives the date, place and circumstances of the
founding of many churches. Fortunately, the New Testament gives a good history of the founding and first years
of the church of Christ. The story of the founding is in

Acts 2, and the first years of its life, teaching and practices are found in the remainder of the New Testament. The church which Christ said He would build was established in Jerusalem on Pentecost, A. D. 30.

Conditions of Membership in His Church

The term "joining the church" is not found in the New Testament. There, men asked what to do to be saved. They were told what to do to be, saved, and did what they were told. Then we read: "And *the Lord added to them* day by day those that were saved" (Acts 2:47).

Plainly, then, the thing to do is to do what the Lord says to do to be saved, and God will add us to the right church, the church of His Son, the Saviour, Christ. Then it is our duty to stay added to the church to which the Lord has added us, and not leave it for anything else. We are to be loyal to it, and serve in it, thus serving Christ as Lord and Master.

We should, therefore, belong to the church, because if we fail to do that which brings us into the church, we have failed to do what we must do to be saved. In the Book of Acts there are given six model conversions, covering about every kind and condition of people—prominent people, good people, bad people, educated people, uneducated people, rich people and poor people. These New Testament examples are found in Acts 2, 8, 9, 10 and 16. Summarizing the answers given in these chapters, we find that they were told to do the following things:

1. Believe in Christ with the whole heart.
2. Repent of their sins toward Christ.
3. Openly confess their faith in Christ.
4. Be buried with Christ by baptism.
5. Continue steadfastly in the faith.

Scriptural Names of the Church

The church is not left for men to name or rename. We find it already named in the Scriptures as follows:

1. The church of Christ (Rom. 16:16).

2. The body of Christ (Col. 1:24; Eph. 4:12 and 5:23).

3. The church of God (Acts 20:28; 1 Cor. 1:2 and 1 Tim. 3:5).

Organization of the Church

The church of Christ, as it is found in the New Testament, consists of saints (members), deacons, elders (bishops). Some of the brethren were set aside to go about and preach the Word, and these were called evangelists. Also, in the first days of the church, there were the twelve apostles, chosen and appointed by the Lord Himself. There were also prophets in the early church. The apostles and prophets have passed away. That leaves us with saints, elders, deacons and evangelists or ministers today.

1. The elders or bishops were to oversee the teaching and spiritual life of the church (1 Timothy 3 and 5. Also, 1 Pet. 5:2, 3 and 1 Thess. 5:12).

2. The character, offices and duties of the deacons are found in Acts 6:1-3 and 1 Tim. 3:8-13.

The Ordinances for the Church and the Rules of Faith and Practice

There is some confusion as to the ordinances to be observed by the church. Again, the Scriptures leave no ground for confusion. The same is true as to its rules of faith and practice.

1. A close examination of the New Testament, reveals two, and only two, ordinances in the church. These were,

and are, baptism and communion—or breaking of bread. These were both definitely ordained by Christ.

2. The New Testament itself is given as a wholly sufficient rule of faith and practice in 2 Tim. 3:16, 17.

CHAPTER IX

THE COMMUNION SERVICE, WHY ATTEND?

"This do in remembrance of me"—Jesus.

Two New Testament Ordinances

There is one New Testament ordinance for those coming into Christ, and one for those who are in Christ.

There are two, and only two, of what are usually referred to as "ordinances" in the New Testament church. One is baptism, and the other is the communion service. One is quite as important as the other. The same Christ commanded both, though some seem to overlook this fact.

Baptism is given as the final means of coming into Christ, and the communion is a means of remaining in Christ by continually remembering and honoring Him.

What the Communion Is Not

To clear up some lack of understanding, we shall first consider one thing that the communion is not. The communion is *not* "a mere form," or a formal part of Christianity. Christ the Saviour died for our sins. The communion service tells that fact. It is the *monument*, the memorial to Him, and the moment we make it a mere form we rob it of everything that it was intended to mean. If we should weep tears over a dead mother, or build a monument to her, *as a mere form,* it would show we had no love at all for her.

[158]

What the Communion Is

The communion service may have other points of meaning which we have failed to enumerate here, but following are some of its meanings:

1. The communion is an ordinance established by the direct and positive command of the Saviour: "This do in remembrance of me" (Luke 22:19, 20).

2. It is an act of worship perpetuated in accordance with one of His last loving requests (Acts 2:42).

3. It is a picture of His death and suffering to be shown to the world until He comes. It is a message preached by symbols (1 Cor. 11:26).

4. It is His table, at which we have an appointment to meet Him, and, through communion with Him, be refreshed and renewed in spirit (Matt. 18:20).

5. It is a test of Christian constancy and loyalty (Heb. 10:23-25).

6. It is a reminder to us of the fact that we are Christians, wearing His name, and pledged to serve Him before the world (Rom. 12:2).

7. It is a memorial, a monument to Him, honoring His name and telling of His death for us (1 Cor. 11:23-26).

8. It is the appointed place for the assembling of Christ's followers. It is the Lord's own appointed way for remembering the Lord on the Lord's Day.

9. It is the central feature of the worship on the first day of the week (Acts 20:7).

10. The elements are emblematic of Christ's body and blood, and in these we are to discern His body and blood (Matt. 26:26-30; 1 Cor. 11:29).

If the communion service is permitted to become a mere form, it loses every one of these named qualities. Its message is obscured, its beauty marred, its purpose defeated.

Importance of Observance

To be faithful to the communion is of supreme importance to every one who is baptized. To neglect it is serious and can easily lead to disaster.

1. If we neglect the communion, we should remember that we are neglecting something founded by Christ and positively commanded by Him.

2. The communion is one of the four essential features of worship in the church of Christ (see Acts 2:42).

They continued steadfastly in four things: (1) The apostles' doctrine; (2) the fellowship (contributions); (3) the breaking of bread (communion), and (4) the prayers.

3. Neglect of the communion brings spiritual sickness and death (1 Cor. 11:26-30).

Who Should Partake of the Communion?

First of all, it is, or should be, plain that the communion table is the Lord's table, to which He has invited those who are His. Clearly, only those who have accepted Him as Lord and Master, are expected to participate in the breaking of bread. In other words, the ordinance of communion follows the ordinance of baptism.

When Should the Communion Be Observed?

There has been a bit of confusion on the matter of when and how often we should observe the communion. Jesus commanded us to observe it, but did not say how often. However, Jesus left many things to be made plain later by the Holy Spirit through the apostles. Here, then, we have clear guidance from apostolic example: "And upon *the first day* of the week, when we were gathered together to break bread" (Acts 20:7). Paul, one of the apostles, was present on this occasion. There is neither command nor apostolic example for the monthly or quarterly communion. There is apostolic example for the communion on the first day of the week.

There are four main features of New Testament worship, as shown in Acts 2:42. All churches include three of these *every* Lord's Day. All teach and preach the doctrine. All have the offerings. All have prayers. Why leave out just one of the four on *any* Lord's Day? The communion should be included in the worship each Lord's Day.

CHAPTER X

WHAT DOES GOD REQUIRE OF ME AS A CHRISTIAN?

"Let him that thinketh he standeth take heed lest he fall"—Paul.

Four Phases of Christian Life

This study will certainly not be an attempt to enumerate all the things which the heavenly Father might require under every kind of circumstance. Even Jesus did not attempt to do that. He merely summed it all up by saying that the first of all comprehensive requirements is that we should love the Lord God with all our heart and soul and mind. He knew that this would cover every condition and contingency. The four phases under which Christian life and activity might be grouped include our Christian worship, our Christian living, Christian service and Christian perseverance.

What Is Required in Worship?

In Acts 2:42 there are mentioned four things in which they continued steadfastly after baptism:

1. "The apostles' doctrine" or teaching. Every real Christian will want and need to know more and more of

God's Word; hence the reading of the Word, the listening to the Word preached, the study of the Word in private and in Bible school.

We should know the doctrine once for all delivered to the saints, until we are thoroughly safeguarded against the confusing religious teachings and irreligious teachings of men. "Know the truth, and the truth shall make you free." "Thy word is truth." Every Christian should study to show himself "approved unto God, a workman that needeth not to be ashamed, rightly dividing the word of truth."

2. They continued steadfastly in the "fellowship." As this word was used, it did not then mean mere social and Christian fraternity. It referred directly to their offerings for the needy and for the church. Too often we look upon the offering as a necessary, but unspiritual, matter. It is one of the four features of worship enumerated in the New Testament, and should be attended by the same conscientious, reverent and worshipful devotion as is fitting for the communion or the prayers.

3. They continued steadfastly in the "breaking of bread." This has been covered in the previous chapter, but we add a word here. Not only should the bread be broken every Lord's Day, but every Christian should make it the first rule of his Christian life never to miss the Lord's Table unless absolutely compelled to do so. The Lord's Day is His. Certainly we ought to give Him at least enough of it so that we might meet with the other Christians to remember the Lord on the Lord's Day in this, the Lord's own appointed way (Acts 20:7).

4. "The prayers." It may take skill or practice to "make a prayer." It takes no skill or practice to "pray." Any Christian can pray a most acceptable prayer to God

in the name of Christ. Study the Lord's prayer as a model. Talk to the heavenly Father as a loving, all-wise and all-powerful and good Father. Begin praying, and keep it up (Matt. 6:9-13; Jas. 5:16; 1 Thess. 5:17).

What Is Required in the Matter of Our Lives?

The New Testament gives principles rather than rules for the guidance of our Christian lives.

1. One of the first things is that we put aside selfishness, and weigh things we do in the light of what is pleasing and helpful to Christ, rather than merely what is pleasing to ourselves (Heb. 13:21).

2. We should weigh things in the light not only of what is hurtful to ourselves, but what is hurtful to the cause of Christ. Will my action cause some one else to stumble and possibly fall? (see Rom. 14:15-21).

3. We are not only to avoid doing that which is hurtful to the cause of Christ, but do everything possible that will be helpful.

4. We are expected to "grow in grace" and in "knowledge of the truth" (2 Pet. 1:5-11).

What of Service?

By serving Christ we best serve ourselves. What reward can there be, here or hereafter, to a life barren of service?

1. "Even as the Son of man came not to be ministered unto, but to minister." A Christian is a follower of Christ. How can we be followers of Him unless we follow Him in service? (Matt. 20:28).

2. The one means by which Christ has planned to save the world is through the service of those who are saved. Shall Christ fail because we, His followers, fail to serve? (Matt. 28:18-20).

3. Service is our own only means of gaining strength. Bible study without service will not make us strong any more than much good food without exercise will make us athletes. "For if ye do these things, ye shall never fall" (2 Pet. 1: 10). Here is promise based on service.

Perseverance

Last of all, God requires perseverance. "Be thou faithful unto death, and I will give thee a crown of life." (Rev. 2: 10). This is the summed-up message of the last book of the Bible. Fortunately, the Saviour does not ask us to succeed. He asks us to try and keep on trying. This, again, is something any one can do. Thus God has given a plan which any one can understand, any one can believe, and any one can follow. He fittingly closes the great book in the last chapter by the great, general invitation to all—to "whosoever will."

On the Lord's Day the Lord's People

Should be in the Lord's House

Around the Lord's Table

To Remember the Lord on the Lord's Day

In the Lord's Own Appointed Way

Section B. Doctrinal Bible-school Opening Exercise

(For Joint General Assembly)

Opening Songs and Prayer.

Responsive Reading.

Primary Supt.—What did Jesus say of little children?

Primary and Beginners Depts.—"Suffer the little children to come unto me, and forbid them not: for of such is the kingdom of God."—Mark 10:14.

Superintendent—What is the first step in the gospel plan of salvation?

All School Above Primary—Faith. "But without faith it is impossible to please him: for he that cometh to God must believe that he is, and that he is a rewarder of them that diligently seek him."—Heb. 11:6.

Assistant Supt.—What is the second step in the gospel plan of salvation?

Boys and Men—Repentance. "Nay: but, except ye repent, ye shall all likewise perish."—Luke 13:3.

Secretary—What is the third step in the gospel plan of salvation?

Girls and Women — Confession. "For with the heart man believeth unto righteousness; and with the mouth confession is made unto salvation."—Rom. 10:10.

Pianist—What is the fourth step in the gospel plan of salvation?

School—Baptism. "Repent, and be baptized every one of you in the name of Jesus Christ for the remission of sins, and ye shall receive the gift of the Holy Ghost."—Acts 2:38.

Orchestra Leader — What is the fifth and last step in the gospel plan of salvation?

Junior Dept.—A godly life as described in Second Peter 1:5-9.

First Intermediate Girls—"And beside this, giving all diligence, add to your faith virtue;

First Intermediate Boys—"And to virtue knowledge;

Second Intermediate Boys—"And to knowledge temperance;

Second Intermediate Girls—"And to temperance patience;

Alpha Class—"And to patience godliness;

Young Men—"And to godliness brotherly kindness;

Young Women—"And to brotherly kindness charity.

Teachers—"For if these things be in you, and abound, they make you that ye shall neither be barren nor unfruitful in the knowledge of our Lord Jesus Christ.

Loyal Men—"But he that lacketh these things is blind, and cannot see afar off, and hath forgotten that he was purged from his old sins."

Loyal Women—"Let love be without dissimulation. Abhor that which is evil; cleave to that which is good."—Rom. 12:9.

Superintendent—"Study to show thyself approved unto God, a workman that needeth not to be ashamed, rightly dividing the word of truth."—2 Tim. 2:15.

School—"Be thou faithful unto death, and I will give thee a crown of life."—Rev. 2:10.

Class Period and Closing.

(To be printed on cardboard, or on paper which can be inserted in songbooks.)

Section C. Doctrinal Charts and Drill

It Is Always **Safe**
To Go by the **Bible**
It Is **Unsafe** to Go by
Anyone or **Anything** Else

The Best **EVIDENCE**
Of Your Faith
In the **WORD** of **GOD**
Is Your Taking **GOD** at His Word

———

"Not Everyone That **SAITH** Unto Me,
Lord, Lord, Shall Enter Into the Kingdom
of Heaven, But He that **DOETH THE WILL**
of My Father Which Is In Heaven" Matt. 7: 21.

———

"**WITHOUT FAITH** It Is **IMPOSSIBLE** to Please Him:
For He **THAT COMETH** to God **MUST BELIEVE** That He Is,
and That He Is a **REWARDER** of Them That **DILIGENTLY
SEEK HIM**" Heb. 11: 6.
"Faith Cometh by **HEARING**, Hearing by the
WORD OF GOD" Rom. 10: 17.

———

"The Times of **IGNORANCE** Therefore
God **OVERLOOKED**; But **NOW**
He **COMMANDETH** Men That They Should
All, **EVERYWHERE REPENT**" (R. V.) Acts 17: 30.

"Whosoever .   Shall **CONFESS ME BEFORE MEN**, Him Will
I **CONFESS ALSO BEFORE MY FATHER** Which
Is In Heaven" Matt. 10: 32.
"With the **MOUTH** Confession Is Made Unto
Salvation" Rom. 10: 10.
"**THOU ART THE CHRIST**, the Son of the
Living God" Matt. 16: 16.

———

"Repent Ye, and **BE BAPTIZED** Every One of You
IN THE NAME OF JESUS CHRIST, Unto the
REMISSION OF YOUR SINS; and Ye Shall
Receive the Gift of the Holy Spirit" (R. V.) Acts 2: 38.

———

"As Many . . . As Have **BEEN BAPTIZED** Into Christ
Have Put **ON CHRIST**" Gal. 3: 27.   "There Is . . . No
CONDEMNATION to Them That Are In Christ Jesus" Rom. 8: 1.
"**THEREFORE** We Are **BURIED** With Him by
BAPTISM" Rom. 6: 4.

———

"**THIS DO** . . . in Remembrance of Me" 1 Cor. 11: 25.
"The **FIRST DAY OF THE WEEK**, . . . we . . . gathered . . .
to **BREAK BREAD**" (R. V.) Acts 20: 7.
"Ye **PROCLAIM THE LORD'S DEATH** Till He Come"
(R. V.) 1 Cor. 11: 26.
"If Ye **DO THESE THINGS**, Ye Shall **NEVER STUMBLE**"
(R. V.) 2 Pet. 1: 10.

———

"**A NAME** Which Is **ABOVE EVERY NAME**" Phil. 2: 9.
"Whatsoever Ye Do, . . . Do All in the **NAME OF THE** Lord"
Col. 3: 17.
"**KEEP THEM IN THY NAME** Which Thou Hast Given Me"
(R. V.) John 17: 11.
"**HIS NAME** Shall Be **IN THEIR FOREHEADS**" Rev. 22: 4.

———

NOTE: Where used for banners, words in capitals should be done in red.

[167]

CHAPTER I

THE RESPONSIBILITY AND THE NEED

Whose Job Is It?

Too often the evangelist has been held responsible for any and all backsliding of converts. When through blaming the evangelist, we next blame the convert himself, forgetting that Scripturally and literally the new convert is a "babe in Christ." Many times the evangelist is able to indoctrinate and teach so thoroughly that the new convert is grounded and fixed so that he will work out his own salvation, whether any later help is given him or not. In many other cases it is wholly impossible for the evangelist to ground all the converts so thoroughly. In any case, the *responsibility* for care and guidance after baptism rests squarely upon the shoulders of the *elders*. Scripturally, the minister is also the evangelist, or an "evangelist," but, as we operate today, our ministers have become largely "full-time elders." In that case the responsibility is upon the minister along with the other elders.

What the Converts Need

Converts to Christ will be different in their needs, depending upon age, past life and present problems.

There are some needs, however that are common. These common needs are: *Food, Exercise* and *Counsel.* They all need these three things. All food and no exercise quickly results in spiritual indigestion and loss of appetite. All counsel and no food or exercise results in failure to develop personal responsibility, discourages growth and leads to spiritual infantile paralysis. All exercise and no food or counsel many times results in much unwise activity, which can become a disturbing force in the whole church. All three phases must be planned for immediately following the meeting.

How Soon Should These Needs Be Provided?

The question often comes up, "How long should we wait before giving the new convert something definite to do, and presenting him with a pledge card on which to indicate his weekly contribution?" Some have hesitated about the first for fear of frightening the new convert and about the latter for fear of offending him. Our answer is, proceed on both these at the earliest possible time, not later than one week after the close of the meeting. The new convert is alert and interested and expects to be asked to have a part in supporting the church. Immediately after the meeting is the psychological time to present the matter. If we put it off for a month or six months he concludes that the church does not need his help, he loses interest, partly because he has no definite part, and then we blame the evangelist or the convert if the convert falls away.

As to work, he should be given something to do immediately after his baptism. Do not wait for the meeting to close. Each new convert is the open gate to another unreached person. Find who that person is and send the new convert to invite him. Let some of the new members help usher. Put some in the choir. Put all of them to work. Certainly, we should not embarrass or scare new members by asking them to do things for which they are wholly unequipped and unprepared. They are certainly not ready to be made elders, deacons, superintendents or teachers. They should be tried, tested and trained for these positions. Neither should they be asked to read in public, pray in public or do other such service until they have been prepared for it. However, there is something each one can do, and our task is to discover what that thing is and ask him to do it.

There is this word of caution. Safeguard the meeting against the overenthusiastic new convert who is insistent on doing something that is hurtful; for instance, playing an instrumental solo on some instrument or singing a solo when his or her efforts are so inferior as to throw cold shivers into a whole audience. Guide as well as suggest.

In the following chapters we give some definite suggestions as to ways by which the provision for these needs may be made.

If Elders Should Do as Much
Real Overseeing as They Do of
Overlooking New Members,
Backsliding Would Be Put on the Skids

CHAPTER II

A DEFINITE PLAN

A Family Gathering

It is important to make the new members feel that
they are really adopted into the church family. A properly conducted reception is an excellent way to achieve
this end. While achieving this end by means of a reception, the proper atmosphere is created in which the enrollment for service and the pledging for support of the
church may be gracefully and successfully presented. Each
suggestion which follows is important, because the combi-
nation creates the family spirit and produces the very
atmosphere desired.

Where Hold the Reception?

A large church parlor or gymnasium or basement is
the best place for a reception. Where these are not available, use the church auditorium if the seats are movable.
The effort should be made to have all old members and
all new members present. Send out a general letter to
all. This is important. Therefore, the place should be
the largest available, so as to accommodate all without
crowding or without being seated formally as they would
have to be in an auditorium with fixed seats.

Arrange the room in imitation of a parlor or reception
room. Ask for an abundance of throw rugs, bridge lamps
and floor lamps. Use plenty of extensions so as to place
these lamps in every corner and down each sideline, as
well as in the center. (See drawing.)

[171]

The White-flower, Circle Service

In the center place a nicely decorated table with lights, flowers and attractive light refreshments, such as fruit-punch and wafers. Decorate generously with crepe paper. Have ladies appointed to prepare this table and to serve when the time comes. On this table have vases of *white* flowers, at least one flower for each new member. (All who have united within the year may be counted as new members.) Around the central table place a circle of chairs facing outward, one for each new member present. Leave a circular passageway, covered with throw rugs, entirely around this circle of chairs. Then place chairs, facing in, entirely around the outer walls, circling at the corners and leaving open only an entry way. These outer chairs are for all members and friends other than the new members. If need be, a double row may be used.

ROOM ARRANGEMENT

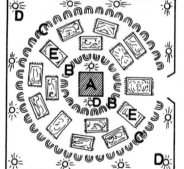

A - Central Table

B - Chairs for New Members

C - Chairs for All Others

D - Bridge Lamps

E - Throw Rugs

Suggested Program

1. Greet new members and seat as shown. Seat both old and new members in family groups.

2. Brief song-service and prayer.

3. Five-minute talk by evangelist or minister and invitation song. Invite any prospects to step from *outer* circle to *inner* circle.

4. Three-minute address of welcome by minister to new converts and introduction of elders with brief explanation of relationship of elders to the new members.

5. Use elders, assisted by little girls, to present a white flower and a pin to each new member, introducing each individual new member as the flower is presented. Minister or evangelist explains significance of the white flower.

6. Presentation of a New Testament to each new member by elders. Have converts' names written in. Minister very briefly explains significance of New Testament.

7. Presentation of packet of contribution envelopes to each new member by church treasurer, assisted by deacons.

8. Inner circle stands and sings one verse of "Oh Happy Day." Minister or evangelist pledges loyalty of new members to Christ, the church and to the leadership of the elders. (They remain standing.)

9. Outer circle stands. Minister pledges elders and all older members to loyalty to Christ, the church and to the new members.

10. The people in each circle join hands and all sing "Blest Be the Tie."

11. All seated. Place cards similar to sample on page 183,* and lead pencils in hands of *every* member, *old* and *new*. Leader takes up item by item as shown on cards. Explain each item and urge *every one* to check. Ask those who already have pledges to note them down on the cards. Ask older members as well as new to check work in which they are participating or will participate.

---

* See page 183 of appendix for form of card to be revised for local needs and locally printed.

12. Brief social program if desired.

13. Serving of refreshments by ladies in charge, serving new members first.

14. General handshaking, final song and benediction.

Immediate Use of Cards*

The cards as checked are of greatest immediate importance. Naturally the treasurer and secretary will want to check at once for records of new pledges, or old pledges increased or decreased. They will find that this evening's work has almost entirely eliminated the need for an every-member canvass.

However, the treasurer should not be allowed to keep these cards for more than one evening. The minister should list by groups, every member who has checked "choir" or "orchestra" or "Christian Endeavor" or "prayer meeting" or any other work. Immediately the elders and other leaders should be given these lists. There is work for every department head to do immediately. Christian Endeavor leaders should immediately contact and enroll those who have checked C. E. The treasurer should send a letter of appreciation to all who have made pledges or increased their pledges. The elders should call at once to acquaint themselves with these new members in their homes. The minister may well express his appreciation to all who have checked for prayer meeting, etc.

Such a reception so conducted will quickly place every member in a position where he can start to work, will take advantage of the psychological moment for engaging the new members in supporting the church, will conserve their interest and will send a new thrill through the whole congregation.

---

* For sample of cards referred to see page 183.

CHAPTER III

OVERSIGHT AND TRAINING BY ELDERS AND MINISTER

A Difference

There is a vast difference between *oversight* and *overlook*. We believe that it is not uncommon for elders to overlook their oversight of the new members. This watchcare is one of their first and most sacred obligations. Many an elder never makes the slightest effort to cultivate or continue any personal acquaintance with the new members. They are quickly lost to him, either in the congregation or in the world to which they may drift back unless attention is given to their nurture and development.

Coming to Know New Members

We believe the elders should make it a first duty and obligation to call in the home of every new member, be he adult or child. This is entirely in addition to anything the minister may do about the matter. If necessary, the list may be divided if it is large, but if elders are to pretend to be shepherds, they must come to know their sheep and lambs, and their sheep and lambs must know them. Whatever method is chosen, the work should by all means be continued until the elders know the members of their flock personally, not only at church, but in the home and on the street.

A Written Memorial

Personally, we would recommend that each new convert be furnished a baptismal certificate and record. There are a number of kinds. Some are inexpensive little booklets which include Scriptural instruction. Others are mere certificates, some of which are gummed for pasting in the new member's Bible. Recently a "membership certificate" has been provided, for presentation to those who have united by letter or statement, to be given out at the same time the baptismal certificates are given to those baptized during the meeting.

Definite Training

With all that may be done in the Bible school, and with all that may be taught during the meeting or included on a printed certificate, there is yet need that definite and special doctrinal teaching be given all new converts, that they may be grounded in the faith.* When this is done, they should then be enrolled, if at all possible, in a training for service class, to prepare them either to teach or to do personal evangelism.

We would add one more word here which comes out of a third of a century of experience. We found that, teach as we would, exhort as we might, iterate and reiterate clear New Testament precepts as we did, yet it failed to sink in and hold all. We did note, however, that those who could be interested to *read* tracts, books and the church paper, were the ones who soon knew the doctrine and were anchored to stay. We, therefore, urge that the church use what means it may see fit to place a good doctrinal church paper in the home of every new member for at least the first year. The cost of such a paper, the cost of the New Testaments given at the reception, and any other like costs, will quickly be taken care of by the contributions made by those giving their pledges at the reception.

---

* The material in Part III, Section A, is excellent for this purpose.

APPENDIX

The following pages contain practical suggestions, for all workers, for printed forms to be printed locally, a Bible drill, drawings and specifications for baptismal robes and a few suggestions for advertising copy.

Some Do's and Do-not's for the Campaign

I. *Evangelist.*

1. Do not expect others to work if you loaf. Set the example in all things.

2. Do not preach big sermons. Use the simple gospel teaching. Do not cheapen the gospel with vulgarities.

3. Do not exhibit ill temper. It's catching.

4. Do not allow a dead or dull minute. Be prepared in a program for each service so that interest is sustained from first to last.

5. Do unto others as ye would that they do unto you. Put yourself in the place of each hearer.

6. Preach the Word. Preach with conviction, sincerity and earnestness. Thus prove that you believe the gospel you preach.

II. *Minister.*

1. Start preparing and planning far ahead of the meeting.

2. Lead. Do not drive.

3. Use tactics not already worn threadbare in your community.

4. Be enthusiastic, earnest, determined and resourceful, but not dictatorial.

5. Work as though you believed that the lost are lost.

III. *Department Leaders.*

1. Do not allow any enterprises, socials or affairs, public or private, to interfere with the meeting. Win the war, then take up the usual enterprises of the church. Put the meeting first.

2. Remember you are a captain. You have been honored by being entrusted as leader of a department. Plan and lead your department so that its whole effort may count for results in the meeting.

3. Shape all your plans so as to fit into the general plan. Work WITH the minister and evangelist.

IV. *Members.*

1. Remember, that after all, it is the members, and not the evangelist, that determine the success of a meeting. It is work and interest on the part of every member that makes the successful meeting. Expect to work, plan to work, then work.

2. Taboo selfishness. Think of the other fellow. Yield your seat to the outsider. Help the ushers. Sit where you are asked instead of where you please. Keep sweet, be gracious to everybody. Seek and greet the stranger. Be willing to be used or abused if it will help to break the barriers of indifference. Watch for every opportunity to say a word to encourage some one to come forward.

3. Do not knock or criticize, publicly or privately. Save your criticism until the campaign is over. You are a member. Your criticism might send some one to torment.

4. Make the meeting first. Arrange not only your social affairs, but your home affairs, so you may be a real helper in the meeting.

5. Never leave the audience while the invitation song is being sung, unless forced to by a crying baby or sudden sickness. By all means do not parade out of the choir, after the service has begun, until the last verse of the invitation is sung and the service concluded. Better stay out entirely than to come and then walk out.

6. Treat the evangelist with all courtesy and hospitality, but do not expect him to sleep in a different bed each night, visit until one o'clock each night, eat two picnic meals each day and then do good work. No man can stand up and do his best work under such misapplied kindness.

7. Help to get these "Do's and Do-nots" over to others.

**PEOPLE WHOM GOD CAN NOT USE
BUT WHOM THE DEVIL DOES USE**

1. The member who says, "It Can't Be Done."
2. Mr. Grouch, Mrs. Gadabout and Mrs. Gossip.
3. The Christian who puts everything else before Christ and the church.
4. The sinful, unrepentant member.
5. The selfish, self-centered member who has no interest in the unsaved.

RELIGIOUS CENSUS RECORD

PLEASE WRITE OR PRINT PLAINLY AND ACCURATELY .... Date data was taken ....

Street or road .... Location on street or road .... City, town or township ....

NAMES		MEMBER OF WHAT CHURCH	CHURCH PREFERENCE	ATTENDS WHAT SUNDAY SCHOOL	WILL ATTEND YES—NO
Husband					
Wife					
Other adults, roomers, etc.					
Other adults, roomers, etc.					
Child's name	Age				
Child's name	Age				
Child's name	Age				
Child's name	Age				

WRITE ADDITIONAL INFORMATION ON BACK OF RECORD .... Name of census worker

---

PROSPECT AND PRAYER LIST

Name of worker ....

Following and on reverse side are names and addresses
of people whom I hope to see won during the campaign.
I will work and pray for these that they may be won.

....

....

....

....

(Over)

MT. WASHINGTON CHURCH OF CHRIST

Being a baptized believer in Christ, and a member of

the .... Church, I wish to have my name
enrolled as a member of the Mt. Washington Church. I

will present this card at the service next ....

Name ....

Address ....

Personal Worker's Name..

MT. WASHINGTON CHURCH OF CHRIST

Being a believer in Christ as the Son of God and only
Saviour, I here and now state my purpose to confess my
faith in Him publicly and obey His command to be baptized at my earliest opportunity. I shall plan to be at

the service next ....

Name ....

Address ....

Cards which may be copied on 3 x 5 white stock. They may be either printed or copied on type-writer. The top one is for listing prospect and prayer lists. The others are for use of personal workers when calling.

CHRISTIAN WORKMEN

Mt. Washington Church of Christ

2 Tim. 2: 15

Every member of this congregation is expected to have part in the work of the church. Please check below the work in which you will agree to help and the services which you will attend regularly.

☐ Bible School   ☐ Teacher or Workers' Training Class

☐ Prayer Meeting   ☐ Calling Committee

☐ Christian Endeavor   ☐ Women's Organizations

☐ Junior or Inter. C. E.   ☐ Mercy and Help Committee

☐ Choir   ☐ Orchestra

This church is supported by the regular weekly contributions of its members. EVERY member should have a regular pledge as large as is consistent with his income. Please write the amount which you will agree to contribute.

Current Expenses .... $........................... Weekly

Missions .... $........................... Weekly

Name ....

Address ....

Telephone ....

Where Employed ....

For explanation of practical use, see pages 173 and 174.

This copy can be adjusted to local needs and reprinted on cards 3 x 5 or larger if desired.

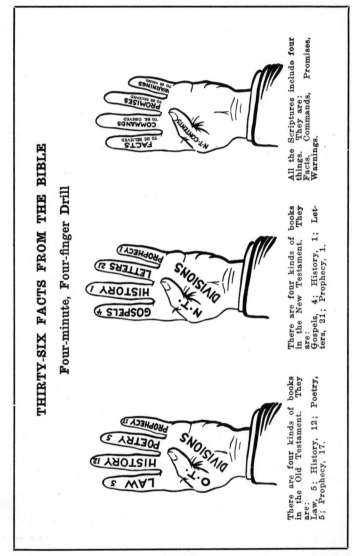

THIRTY-SIX FACTS FROM THE BIBLE

Four-minute, Four-finger Drill

There are four kinds of books in the Old Testament. They are: Law, 5; History, 12; Poetry, 5; Prophecy, 17.

There are four kinds of books in the New Testament. They are: Gospels, 4; History, 1; Letters, 21; Prophecy, 1.

All the Scriptures include four things. They are: Facts, Commands, Promises, Warnings.

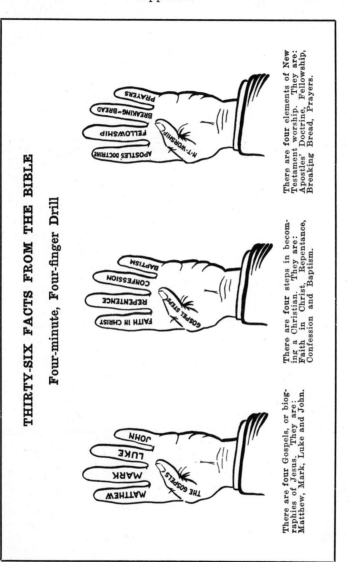

THIRTY-SIX FACTS FROM THE BIBLE

Four-minute, Four-finger Drill

There are four Gospels, or biographies of Jesus. They are: Matthew, Mark, Luke and John.

There are four steps in becoming a Christian. They are: Faith in Christ, Repentance, Confession and Baptism.

There are four elements of New Testament worship. They are: Apostles' Doctrine, Fellowship, Breaking Bread, Prayers.

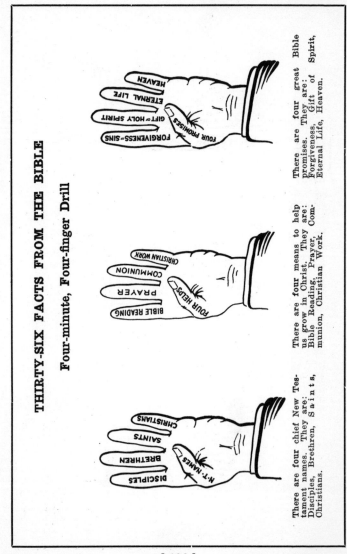

THIRTY-SIX FACTS FROM THE BIBLE

Four-minute, Four-finger Drill

There are four chief New Testament names. They are: Disciples, Brethren, Saints, Christians.

There are four means to help us grow in Christ. They are: Bible Reading, Prayer, Communion, Christian Work.

There are four great Bible promises. They are: Forgiveness, Gift of Spirit, Eternal Life, Heaven.

Drawing of Baptismal Robe

Figure I

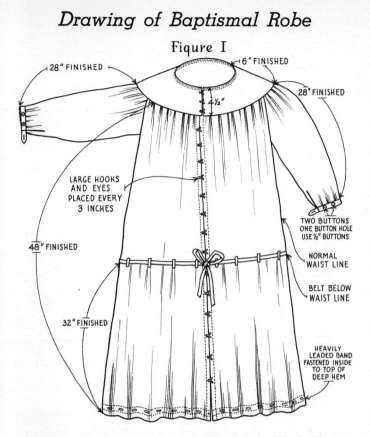

28" FINISHED

6" FINISHED

28" FINISHED

4½"

LARGE HOOKS AND EYES PLACED EVERY 3 INCHES

TWO BUTTONS ONE BUTTON HOLE USE ½" BUTTONS

NORMAL WAIST LINE

BELT BELOW WAIST LINE

48" FINISHED

32" FINISHED

HEAVILY LEADED BAND FASTENED INSIDE TO TOP OF DEEP HEM

Drawing and Measurements of Baptismal Robe Which Meets All Demands for Making Baptism a Burial

Economical because the same robe is adjustable for either men or women; for tall people or for short people; thin people or heavy people.

Perfectly simple to make. No pattern needed except for the yoke. Follow measurements and instructions.

Cloth suggested has been chosen from many, by actual tests, because it meets the requirements of nonabsorbence, lets air pass out through mesh readily, drapes automatically, is nonclinging, does not mildew, is thoroughly opaque and stands the wetting and drying indefinitely. No cotton cloth will meet these tests.

A church equipped with these robes is ever prepared for a baptism, because they are so built that no undergarments are necessary, except stockings.

While white is never suitable for adult robes, it is permissible for children's robes, which may be made after the same pattern, merely reducing measurements.

Detailed Drawings for Baptismal Robe

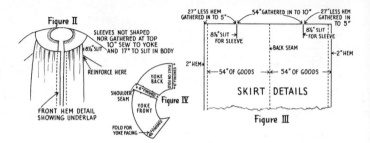

Detailed Instructions for Baptismal Robe

1. Use **DARK**-colored material. Strictly **FAST** color.

2. Do **NOT** use white—
   It becomes transparent when wet.
   It soon stains, and appears soiled.
   It emphasizes, rather than obscures, bodily form.

3. Wool crepe material is preferable. Costs about $1.00 a yard.

4. Use 4½ yards of 54-inch material, or 7 yards of 36-inch. 54-inch cuts to better advantage.

5. Cut yoke so as to be 6 inches deep at back and shoulders when finished. Cut out front of neck to 4½ inches finished. Completely line yoke with sateen to reinforce it. Figure IV.

6. **Skirt—Figure III.**
   Cut cloth 52 inches long. Use two full breadths of 54-inch goods or three breadths of 36-inch. Put three-inch hem at bottom. Divide top into four equal parts with uniting seam at center of back. Gather the back 54-inches into ten inches. Split the cloth down 8½ inches, 27 inches from the front, for making sleeve openings. Gather each front section in to 5 inches.

7. Front opening hems should be two inches wide and strong, one of which should protrude to constitute a flap under front opening hem. See Figure II.

8. **Sleeve detail.**
   Cut off 28 inches of 54-inch material. Split in the middle, making two 27-inch widths. Do not shape the shoulder. Loose blousing effect takes care of shaping. Ten inches of top of sleeve is sewed to ten inches of end of yoke. Remaining 17 inches is sewed to 8½ inch split in skirt. Gather lower part of sleeve in to ten inches. Fasten to 12-inch sleeve band with two inches serving as button-hole flap. Figure I.

9. Use **only** large hooks and eyes on front, at three-inch intervals. Do **not** use snaps. They fail at critical moments. Do **not** use **buttons**. The buttonholes eventually stretch. Figure I.

10. Make belt of same material, ¾-inch wide when finished, 108 inches long.

11. Set belt 32 inches up from bottom of hem. Figure I.

12. Use much more weight than seems necessary. Air in skirt will have heavy lift Use 216 inches of 1¼-inch binding tape, sewed together into double band. Get piece of sheet lead and cut into pieces 2 x ½-inch. Sew these inside of band with cross seams to keep from creeping. Sew this band to top of bottom hem on inside of skirt. Figure I.

13. If white is insisted upon, for its significance, use white caps similar to Oriental headdress over white bathing caps for the head, and white jabot under the dark robe, for neck and bust.

Suggestions for Advertising

Design for hand-painted banner, ten feet by three feet. See suggestions in paragraph 5 on page 65. Use red for large "R."

Suggestions for signs to be carried on rear of automobiles.

CHURCH ON FIRE
WITH GOSPEL ENTHUSIASM

Spreading Rapidly Over
the Neighborhood

Great crowds are attending every night to hear the Bible drills, old-time songs and the sermons of Evangelist J. H. Jones. You'll enjoy it all if you are one of the many present tonight.

Suggestion for display ad to be used in newspaper. Same can be used on a dodger or in the church bulletin. Can be hand-drawn on large banner if desired. For newspaper work, use cut of your own building.

[189]